Basic English Grammar

by
Bonnie L. Walker

AGS®
American Guidance Service, Inc.
Circle Pines, Minnesota 55014-1796
800-328-2560

About the Author

Bonnie L. Walker taught for sixteen years in secondary schools and college. She holds a Ph.D. in curriculum theory and instructional design from the University of Maryland, an M.Ed. in secondary education, and a B.A. in English. She studied psycholinguistics at the University of Illinois Graduate School and was a curriculum developer at the Model Secondary School for the Deaf at Gallaudet University. She is the author of *Basic English Composition, Life Skills English,* and numerous workbooks, learning packages, and sound filmstrips in written expression, grammar, and usage. She was a member of Project EduTech, which investigated promising technologies to improve the delivery of special education services. Dr. Walker has written several papers on the applications of personal computers, video technology, and cable television in education. She has been the director for research and development projects funded by the U.S. Department of Education, the U.S. Department of Agriculture, and the Administration on Youth, Children, and Families. Since 1986, Dr. Walker has been president of a research and development company specializing in development of training and educational materials for special populations.

Photo Credits: pp. viii, 190—James L. Shaffer; pp. 2, 26, 78, 110, 152, 196—Patterson Graphics; p. 52—Eugen Gebhardt/FPG International; p. 92—John Terence Turner/FPG International; pp. 128, 254—Cathlyn Melloan/Tony Stone Images; pp. 172, 198, 298—Superstock; p. 220—Jim and Mary Whitmer; p. 274—David Young-Wolff/Tony Stone Images

Printed in the United States of America

ISBN 0-7854-2308-7 (Previously ISBN 0-7854-0495-3)

Product Number 91380

A 0 9 8 7 6 5 4 3

Contents

Part 1

Why Study Grammar?

No matter what kind of writing you do, you need to know how words work in sentences. In other words, you need good grammar skills. Studying grammar teaches you the rules about putting the right words in the right places in sentences.

Knowing grammar will help you write clearly so that your reader will understand exactly what you are trying to say. Once you know the rules about how to use words, writing will become much easier. You won't have to think about whether your words are right. Just like riding a bicycle or driving a car, your use of words will become automatic.

When you study grammar, you will learn that every word in a sentence has a purpose. The English language has thousands of words. Each of these words can be put into at least one of eight main groups. These groups are called parts of speech.

Parts of Speech

Nouns	Words that name people, places, things, and ideas.
Pronouns	Words that replace nouns.
Adjectives	Words that describe nouns or pronouns.
Verbs	Words that express action or a state of being in a sentence.
Adverbs	Words that tell about the action. They can tell how, when, where, or how much.
Prepositions	Words that show relationships between a noun and the rest of the sentence.
Conjunctions	Words that connect sentences or parts of a sentence.
Interjections	Words that express feelings.

In Part 1 of this book, you will learn about the different parts of speech. You will learn how to recognize the parts of speech in sentences. You will also learn how to use the different parts of speech effectively and correctly in sentences of your own.

Chapter 1

The Noun

Stores advertise the names of products to buy. Newspapers include the names of people, places, things, and ideas. No matter where you are, you find that everything and everyone in the world has a name. Things and people need names so that everyone can talk about them more easily.

A noun is a word that names a person, place, thing, or idea.

In Chapter 1, you will learn about nouns. Each lesson is about the different types of nouns used in everyday speech and writing.

Goals for Learning

▶ To identify nouns in sentences

▶ To identify proper nouns in sentences

▶ To write the plural form of nouns

▶ To write the possessive form of nouns

Noun

Names a person, place, thing, or idea.

A **noun** is a word that names a person, place, thing, or idea.

EXAMPLES		
	Person:	The insurance **agent** sold Alex a policy.
	Place:	Most **states** require car owners to have insurance.
	Thing:	Alex saved his **money** and bought a **car**.
		The **door** was squeaky, but Alex fixed it.
	Idea:	Alex had to make a **decision**.
		It took **time** to decide.

Activity A Write ten nouns on your paper to go with each group of nouns listed below. Two examples are given in parentheses.

1) time (day, second)

2) places (garage, city)

3) things (book, coat)

4) amounts (size, liter)

5) events (concert, party)

6) persons (student, man)

7) actions (race, trip)

8) qualities (honesty, trust)

Common noun

Names a general type of person, place, thing, or idea.

A **common noun** is the name of a general type of person, place, thing, or idea.

A **proper noun** is the name of a particular person, place, thing, or idea.

Proper noun

Names a particular person, place, thing, or idea.

A common noun is capitalized only if it is the first word of a sentence or part of a title. A proper noun is always capitalized.

EXAMPLES	Common Nouns	Proper Nouns
	president	George Washington
	athlete	Roberto Clemente
	team	Chicago Bulls
	book	*Robinson Crusoe*
	director	Steven Spielberg
	place	Alaska
	day	Tuesday
	document	the Constitution
	movie	*Jurassic Park*

Activity B Write these nouns on your paper. Write a proper noun beside each common noun. Write a common noun beside each proper noun.

Examples president — John F. Kennedy

Canada — country

1) teacher

2) city

3) holiday

4) dog

5) river

6) player

7) team

8) newspaper

9) neighbor

10) singer

11) street

12) band

13) month

14) Ireland

15) Bugs Bunny

16) World Series

17) French

18) Atlantic Ocean

19) Ohio

20) *Star Wars*

Activity C Write these nouns on your paper. Capitalize the proper nouns. A proper noun names a particular person, place, thing, or idea.

1) school
2) actor
3) florida
4) ocean
5) michael j. fox
6) brazil
7) lake
8) july
9) mars
10) england
11) james
12) road
13) america
14) paper
15) katharine hepburn
16) christmas
17) mr. wong
18) carpenter
19) california
20) wednesday
21) planet
22) movie
23) michael jordan
24) high school
25) cal ripken
26) colorado river
27) book
28) miami
29) singer
30) rocky mountains

The name of a particular place is a proper noun. The name of a country, state, city, street, or building is a proper noun.

EXAMPLES	Common Nouns	Proper Nouns
	city	New York City, Los Angeles
	river	the Mississippi River
	street	Main Street
	apartment	Apartment 103
	route	Route 96
	high school	Montgomery High School
	park	Rock Creek Park

Activity D Write these sentences on your paper. Capitalize the proper nouns. Every sentence will have at least one proper noun.

1) Roberto mailed a package to houston, texas.

2) His friend lives at 602 river drive, apartment 119.

3) Last year roberto went to a new high school.

4) He liked northview senior high very much.

5) Roberto and sue went swimming in the lake.

6) The lake was at the end of south shore drive.

7) I met Josie at the corner of schoolhouse road and high street.

8) Our plane was supposed to land in atlanta, georgia.

9) Because of the storm, the pilot announced that we would land in memphis, tennessee.

10) Mayor Johnson invited the band from the james middle school to march in the parade.

An abbreviation is a short form of a word. If the whole word is a proper noun, the abbreviation is capitalized.

EXAMPLES	Proper Noun	Abbreviation
	Maryland	MD
	Doctor Smith	Dr. Smith
	Main Street	Main St.

Activity E   Most of the words in an address are proper nouns. Write these addresses on your paper. Capitalize all of the proper nouns. Abbreviate the names of streets and states when possible.

1) mr. joe keller
route 2, box 206
marshall, iowa 50152

2) mrs. karen blackhorse
99 norris avenue
waterloo, new york 13165

3) mr. c. j. diaz
1580 eaton way
burke, virginia 22015

4) ms. dionne williams
41 maple lane
lyon, california 94104

5) ms. holli rezek
3189 regent street
ocean springs, mississippi 39564

6) mr. sumio nishimura
143 stonesboro drive
apartment 8B
louisville, kentucky 40229

Parts of the country are proper nouns. Directions are common nouns.

EXAMPLES

Part of the country: I visited the **South** last spring.

Direction: I am going **south** next spring.

Activity F   Write these sentences on your paper. Capitalize the proper nouns. Not every sentence will have a proper noun.

1) When alex graduated from high school, he took a trip to the south.

2) On the first day, he drove 300 miles southwest.

3) He started in baltimore and spent the first night in north carolina.

4) On the second day, alex drove west to visit some friends in tennessee.

5) The next day alex headed southeast to florida.

6) I've never been west of the mississippi river.

7) Next year, we plan to take a trip to the west.

8) We'll fly to california and then rent a car.

9) After we visit local sights, we'll drive north to san francisco.

10) My cousins from the northern part of the state will join us on a tour of the southwest.

11) I met hector's uncle who lives in the northeast.

12) Their house is located in the northeastern part of vermont.

The name of a language and a particular course are proper nouns. The name of a subject is a common noun.

EXAMPLES	Proper Nouns	Common Nouns
	English, Spanish	language
	History I	social studies
	Introduction to Biology	science

Activity G   Write the word or words that should appear in each sentence to make it correct.

1) Karl got an A in (English, english).

2) Next year Alex is taking (math and social studies, Math and Social Studies).

3) Jennifer signed up for (math I, Math I).

4) Ima enjoys (physical education, Physical Education).

5) Danny is going on a field trip in (earth science II, Earth Science II).

6) Who teaches your (science, Science) class this year?

7) The students in (drama II, Drama II) will put on a play for their class project.

8) Miguel decided to take (introduction to music, Introduction to Music) for extra credit.

9) Kuri speaks (japanese, chinese, and french; Japanese, Chinese, and French).

10) Did you do better in (geography or history, Geography or History)?

11) Joanie had to choose between (american history I or world history II, American History I or World History II).

12) Our (italian, Italian) teacher does not let us speak (english, English) during class.

A title is a proper noun. Books, songs, movies, and people are some of the things that can have a title. The first word and all main words in a title are capitalized.

EXAMPLES

Reverend Frank Garcia   *Lord of the Rings*

"The Star-Spangled Banner"   *The Red Pony*

Activity H Write these titles on your paper. Capitalize the first word and all main words.

1) *the red badge of courage*
2) *the sound of music*
3) *the tonight show*
4) *the world almanac*
5) president andrew jackson

Activity I Write these sentences on your paper. Capitalize the proper nouns.

1) On wednesday alex came home from florida.
2) His sister jennifer was watching television.
3) "Hello, alex," jennifer said. "Welcome home from the south."
4) "Your boss, mr. wilson, called you yesterday," Jennifer told him.
5) "He wants you to report to the office on millstream drive tomorrow."
6) "Thanks," alex said. "Why are you home? I thought you were taking a french class."
7) "The class meets in the morning. How about taking me for a ride in your new car? I'd like to go south myself."
8) "OK," alex agreed. "Let's go."

Collective noun	A **collective noun** is the name of a group of people or things.
Names a group of people or things.	

> **EXAMPLES**
>
> Groups of people: group, audience, crowd
>
> Groups of things: herd, flock, collection

Activity J   Find five nouns that name a group of things or people in these sentences. Write them on your paper.

1) The baseball team practiced every day.

2) Alex's club had a meeting every Thursday.

3) The whole neighborhood went to the picnic.

4) Carla decided to join the navy.

5) The jury found the man innocent.

Compound noun	The names of people or things may be compound. **Compound**
A noun that is more than one word.	**nouns** may be written as two or more words. Sometimes the words are written separately. Sometimes hyphens are used.

> **EXAMPLES**
>
> | White House | son-in-law | high school |
> |---|---|---|
> | Dr. An Chin | Maple Street | Secretary of State |

Activity K   Write all the nouns in these sentences on your paper.

1) A forget-me-not is a lovely blue flower.

2) The vice president spoke at our graduation.

3) Denali National Park is in Alaska.

4) Anita was the maid-of-honor at the wedding.

5) Kim stuffed jeans and a sweatshirt in her backpack.

A noun may be abstract or concrete.

A **concrete noun** is a word that names something you can see or touch.

An **abstract noun** is a word that names something you can think about or talk about. You cannot see it or touch it. An abstract noun is an idea.

EXAMPLES	Concrete Nouns	Abstract Nouns
	money	cost
	clock	time
	school	education
	steel	strength

Activity L   Write the abstract noun in each pair of words on your paper.

1) fever   thermometer

2) law   judge

3) price   price tag

4) pizza   hunger

5) year   calendar

6) earthquake   disaster

7) kindness   friend

8) telephone   communication

9) tears   disappointment

10) fame   actor

Part A   Write all the nouns in these sentences on your paper. Write whether each noun is *common, proper, concrete, abstract,* or *collective.*

1) Alex Jones wanted a car very much.

2) Every week he saved a certain amount of money.

3) He put his money in a bank and received interest.

4) A decision about a car would not be easy.

5) He wanted a small car that would get good mileage.

6) Alex saw an ad in the newspaper.

7) He called the phone number and made an appointment.

8) Alex looked at automobiles for weeks.

9) Then he found the perfect car. The price was right.

10) Alex had a good feeling. He trusted the seller.

Part B   Write the nouns in these sentences on your paper.

1) Last month Alex got another part-time job.

2) He needed the money to keep his car on the road.

3) His state requires car owners to buy insurance.

4) Alex had to choose among several different plans.

5) The cost was high, but Alex got full coverage.

Singular noun

Names one person, place, thing, or idea.

Plural noun

Names more than one person, place, thing, or idea.

A **singular noun** is the name of one person, place, thing, or idea.

A **plural noun** is the name of more than one person, place, thing, or idea.

Most plural nouns end in -s or -es. When the plural noun ends in -es, the plural has an extra syllable. You can hear the difference if you say the words aloud.

EXAMPLES	Singular Nouns		Plural Nouns	
	ship	group	ships	groups
	quiz	church	quizzes	churches
	dish	six	dishes	sixes

Activity A   Write the plural of each singular noun on your paper. Add either an -s or -es. Say the plural aloud. You will hear the extra syllable when the plural noun ends in -es.

Examples   town — towns   guess — guesses

1) bunch   **5)** school   **9)** wish   **13)** patch

2) address   **6)** ladder   **10)** bush   **14)** icicle

3) car   **7)** mountain   **11)** idea   **15)** sled

4) fox   **8)** ax   **12)** tax   **16)** quiz

Activity B   Number your paper 1–16. Next to each number, write whether the word is *singular* or *plural*.

1) action   **5)** reports   **9)** crowds   **13)** circus

2) bosses   **6)** address   **10)** doctor   **14)** committee

3) team   **7)** majority   **11)** Alex   **15)** women

4) nations   **8)** agents   **12)** monsters   **16)** Elm Street

Nouns that end in -y and have a consonant before the -y become plural by changing the -y to -i and adding -es.

Nouns that end in -y and have a vowel before the -y become plural by simply adding an -s.

EXAMPLES

Nouns That Change		Nouns That Do Not Change	
city	cities	key	keys
lady	ladies	alley	alleys
spy	spies	boy	boys

Activity C   Write these nouns on your paper. Beside each noun, write its plural.

Examples   turkey — turkeys   county — counties

1) monkey

2) chimney

3) country

4) body

5) journey

6) injury

7) army

8) navy

9) bay

10) day

Activity D   Find the spelling mistakes in these sentences. Write the sentences correctly on your paper.

1) Both countrys had spys in their armys.

2) He received keys to two of the citys he visited on his journey.

3) The doctor said their injurys were not serious.

The plural of most nouns that end in *-f* or *-fe* is made by adding *-s*.

EXAMPLES	roof	roofs		chief	chiefs

Some nouns that end in *-f* or *-fe* change the *-f* to *-v* and add *-s* or *-es*.

EXAMPLES	leaf	leaves		calf	calves
	knife	knives		wolf	wolves

The plural of some nouns ending with a consonant and an *-o* is formed by adding *-es*. Others add only the *-s*.

EXAMPLES	hero	heroes		photo	photos
	tomato	tomatoes		hairdo	hairdos

The plural of nouns ending with a vowel and an *-o* is formed by adding *-s*.

EXAMPLES	radio	radios		rodeo	rodeos

A few nouns become plural by changing letters within the word.

EXAMPLES	man	men		foot	feet
	mouse	mice		woman	women
	tooth	teeth		goose	geese

Some singular and plural nouns are spelled the same.

EXAMPLES	deer		sheep
	trout		series

Activity E   Find the spelling mistakes in these sentences. Write the sentences correctly on your paper.

1) Two deers surprised the mans in the woods.

2) The rancher bought eighty sheeps.

3) We went fishing and caught seven trouts.

4) The Reds won two World Serieses in a row.

5) They ate two loafs of bread and ten potatos.

Activity F   Write the plural of each singular noun on your paper. Then write a sentence using each plural noun.

Example   goose — geese   The geese honked as they flew.

1) calf

2) belief

3) foot

4) man

5) tooth

6) child

7) team

8) knife

9) lady

10) monkey

11) tomato

12) potato

13) mouse

14) hero

15) deer

16) chief

17) bus

18) moose

19) woman

20) elf

Part A Find six plural nouns in this paragraph. Write them in order on your paper.

> The traffic in front of the house was heavy for about two hours. About twenty people came to the party. Everyone seemed to be wearing new clothes. The guests stood in small groups around the snacks and around the stereo. They talked about their summer fun and the year to come.

Part B Write the plural of each noun on your paper.

1) woman	**9)** child	**17)** path
2) sheep	**10)** city	**18)** agent
3) goose	**11)** tax	**19)** party
4) tomato	**12)** policy	**20)** knife
5) life	**13)** dish	**21)** trout
6) hero	**14)** potato	**22)** mouse
7) key	**15)** address	**23)** stereo
8) spy	**16)** deer	**24)** business

Part C Write the word that should appear in each sentence to make it correct.

1) In six months, Hector grew two (inchs, inches).

2) There are many large (citys, cities) along the east coast of the United States.

3) Tom's (feet, feets) were sore after the five-mile hike.

4) These (tomatoes, tomatos) will make the salad taste better.

5) My brother had two (cavitys, cavities) filled at the dentist.

| Possessive noun

Shows ownership or relationship. | A **possessive noun** is one that shows ownership or a relationship. A possessive noun ends in *-s* and has an apostrophe. |

| EXAMPLES | Ownership: | That car belongs to Alex.
That is **Alex's** car. |
| | Relationship: | Jennifer is the sister of Alex.
Jennifer is **Alex's** sister. |

Remember that most plural nouns end in *-s* or *-es*. A noun that is possessive also ends in *-s*. Plurals and possessive nouns sound the same when they are said aloud. Many people get plurals and possessives mixed up when they write them. A written possessive noun looks different from a plural noun. The possessive noun uses an apostrophe. Look at the examples below. Notice the difference in the meaning.

EXAMPLES	**Plural Noun**	**Possessive Noun**
	We bought two **tapes**.	He can't find the **tape's** case.
	I read three interesting **books**.	The **book's** author autographed it.
	The **planes** had engine trouble.	The **plane's** engine failed.

Activity A   Write the word in bold in these sentences on your paper. Beside each word, write whether it is *plural* or *possessive*.

Example   Chicago has some of the **world's** tallest buildings.
world's — possessive

1) **Alex's** insurance policy came in the mail.
2) The policy had several **pages**.
3) A few of Alex's **friends** stopped by the house.
4) They came to see their **friend's** new car.
5) They went out to inspect the **car's** tires.
6) The **tires** were brand new.

A possessive noun can be singular or plural. Study the examples below.

Make a singular noun possessive by adding -'s.

Singular	Singular Possessive
teacher	teacher's desk
child	child's bike

Make a plural noun that ends in -s possessive by adding only an apostrophe.

Plural	Plural Possessive
teachers	teachers' meeting
trees	trees' leaves

When a plural noun does not end in -s, make it possessive by adding -'s.

Plural	Plural Possessive
men	men's department
children	children's room

Activity B Write the possessive nouns in these sentences on your paper. Beside each possessive noun, write whether it is *singular* or *plural*.

Example The **ladies'** department had a sale. **ladies'**—plural

1) The monkeys' fur was black.
2) The cat slept on the sofa's cushion.
3) Alex had to replace the camera's batteries.
4) The mice's tracks led under the baseboard.
5) Last week the children's room was painted.

Activity C Write the singular possessive form and the plural possessive form for these words on your paper.

Examples club   club's   clubs'   lady   lady's   ladies'

1) chapter
2) agent
3) person
4) state
5) fox
6) president
7) child
8) church
9) crowd
10) navy

11) job
12) thing
13) noun
14) goose
15) wife
16) audience
17) man
18) foot
19) sunflower
20) county

A number of common expressions contain possessive forms. Many refer to time or to price.

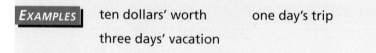

EXAMPLES   ten dollars' worth   one day's trip

three days' vacation

Activity D Write the word that should appear in each sentence to make it correct.

1) Mark likes to put in his two (cents', cent's) worth.
2) Alex gets two (weeks', week's) vacation every year.
3) You will only have a (minutes', minute's) wait.
4) I'd like five (dollar's, dollars') worth of stamps.
5) We hoped for a rest at the (week's, weeks') end.

Part A   Write the possessive nouns in these sentences on your paper. Add apostrophes where they are needed.

1) Alexs job is very important to him.

2) He has worked in Mr. Wilsons store for one year.

3) Mr. Wilson sells mens sports clothes.

4) Every week at the salespersons meeting, they talk about their work.

5) Mr. Wilsons plan is to make Alex a manager some day.

Part B   Some nouns in these sentences are in bold. Write them on your paper. Beside each noun, write whether it is a *plural noun* or a *possessive noun*. Add an apostrophe if it is needed.

Example   Several **years** ago, Jennifer and Alex went to New York.

         years—plural noun (no apostrophe is needed)

1) Jennifer and Alex went to New York City with their **parents**.

2) They wanted to see some of the **worlds** tallest buildings.

3) **Alexs** favorite place was the Statue of Liberty.

4) One of the **familys** most enjoyable places was Lincoln Center.

5) On their way to lunch, they saw a **womens** street band.

6) A street juggler and a mime had them in **stitches**.

7) The **crowds** of people and the subways were exciting.

8) At the **trips** end, they were sorry to leave the city.

Part C   Write the word that should appear in each sentence to make it correct.

1) He got ten (dollars, dollars') worth of gas.

2) My (sisters, sister's) boyfriend is coming for dinner.

3) The (monkeys, monkey's) chattering made everyone laugh.

4) We drove to work in (Alexs, Alex's) new car.

Part A   Write the nouns in these sentences on your paper. Be sure to include possessive nouns.

1) The party was over.

2) Alex and Jennifer let their parents go into the room.

3) Mrs. Jones looked at the living room.

4) Glasses, empty bowls, and dishes were everywhere.

5) Alex and Jennifer cleaned up their friends' mess.

Part B   Write all of the proper nouns in these sentences. Capitalize any proper nouns that are not capitalized.

1) The summer was almost over. In august, Jennifer and Alex would both return to school.

2) Jennifer was going to be a senior at jackson high school.

3) Alex was going to hanover community college.

4) He also planned to work part-time at mr. wilson's store.

5) Jennifer was taking french, math, and science.

6) Alex was taking english and business subjects.

7) Alex remembered his trip to the south.

8) When his english teacher asked him to write a composition, he had a good topic.

9) He decided to title his paper, "my first trip to florida."

10) Alex was proud when ms. romero chose to read his paper aloud to the class.

Part C   Write the plural form of each of these singular nouns.

1) wolf	5) student	9) child
2) city	6) monkey	10) tooth
3) quiz	7) house	
4) teacher	8) party	

Part D Write the word that should appear in each sentence to make it correct.

1) Alex and his friend (miguel, Miguel) went to the movies.

2) They were seeing (*star wars, Star Wars*) for the fifth time.

3) The theater had special prices on (wednesday, Wednesday).

4) They were going to the (Early Show, early show).

5) Alex had to study for an (english, English) test.

6) Miguel also went to (hanover community college, Hanover Community College).

7) Miguel was taking (Basic Computers I, basic computers I).

8) He planned to become a (computer operator, Computer Operator).

9) On the way home there was a lot of (traffic, traffics).

10) Alex and Miguel talked about their (colleges, college's) team.

11) They wondered about the (teams', team's) chances.

12) When they got home, (Alexs, Alex's) sister was waiting.

13) Miguel had been one of (Jennifer's, Jennifers) friends for years.

14) "Did you get your (money's, moneys) worth?" Jennifer asked.

15) "Yes. It is the (worlds, world's) best movie!" he said.

Test Taking Tip Do not wait until the night before a test to study. Plan your study time so that you can get a good night's sleep the night before a test.

Chapter 2

The Pronoun

You talk with people every day in school, at work, in the community, and at home. When you do, you often use the person's name. You talk about the things you do and the thoughts you have.

Whenever you speak or write, you use nouns to name the person or thing you are telling about. When you want to refer to that person or thing again, you can repeat the noun, or you can use a pronoun. A pronoun is a word used in place of a noun.

In Chapter 2, you will learn how to recognize and use pronouns. Each lesson in the chapter focuses on different types of pronouns and their correct use in writing and speaking.

Goals for Learning

▶ To identify pronouns in sentences

▶ To identify the type of pronoun such as personal, indefinite, relative, and demonstrative

▶ To identify correct usage of pronouns in sentences

Pronoun

A part of speech that takes the place of a noun.

A **pronoun** is a word that replaces a noun. Without pronouns, you would have to repeat the same nouns over and over again.

>
>
> Susan said that Susan was going to call Susan's mother.
>
> Susan said that **she** was going to call **her** mother.

Antecedent

The noun that a pronoun replaces.

Every pronoun has an **antecedent**. The antecedent is the noun to which the pronoun refers. The pronoun must agree with the antecedent in number and gender.

> EXAMPLE
>
> **Ellis** is a senior.
>
> **He** is on the track team.
>
> (**Ellis** is the antecedent for the pronoun **he**.)

Personal pronoun

A pronoun that takes the place of a noun and that refers to a person or object.

Personal pronouns distinguish among the speaker, the person spoken to, and the person or thing spoken about.

A first person pronoun refers to the speaker.

>
>
> **I** am late.

A second person pronoun refers to the person spoken to.

> EXAMPLE
>
> **You** are late.

A third person pronoun refers to the person or thing spoken about.

> EXAMPLE
>
> **He** is late.

Personal pronouns express number. They can be singular or plural.

EXAMPLES	**Singular** (one)	**Plural** (more than one)
	I am late.	**We** are late.
	She is leaving.	**They** are leaving.

Personal pronouns express gender. The three genders are *masculine* (male), *feminine* (female), and *neuter* (those that are neither masculine nor feminine).

EXAMPLES	Masculine:	**He** is tall.
	Feminine:	**She** is my friend.
	Neuter:	**It** is a notebook.

Nominative pronoun

A pronoun used as the subject of a sentence.

Objective pronoun

A pronoun used as the object of a sentence.

Possessive pronoun

A pronoun that shows ownership or relationship.

Personal pronouns express case. The case reflects the way the pronoun is used in a sentence.

A pronoun may be used in the **nominative** case as the subject of the sentence, in the **objective** case as an object in the sentence, or in the **possessive** case to show ownership.

EXAMPLES	Nominative:	**He** is in my Spanish class. (subject)
	Objective:	**I** gave it to **him**. (object of the preposition *to*)
	Possessive:	That book is **hers**.

Personal Pronouns			
	Nominative	**Objective**	**Possessive**
Singular			
First person	I	me	my, mine
Second person	you	you	your, yours
Third person	he, she	him, her	his, her, hers
	it	it	its
Plural			
First person	we	us	our, ours
Second person	you	you	your, yours
Third person	they	them	their, theirs

Activity A   Write a pronoun for each numbered item on your paper. Use the chart above for help.

Examples   first person, singular, nominative — **I**

second person, plural, possessive — **your, yours**

third person, singular, objective, masculine — **him**

1) third person, plural, nominative

2) third person, singular, objective, neuter

3) first person, plural, possessive

4) second person, singular, objective

5) third person, plural, possessive

6) first person, singular, objective

7) second person, singular, possessive

8) second person, plural, nominative

Activity B   Rewrite each of these sentences on your paper. Replace the words in bold with a pronoun.

Example   I saw **Mary** yesterday.

I saw **her** yesterday.

1) I have **a hammer and a saw**.

2) **The gloves** are lost.

3) **An airplane** is flying overhead.

4) I wrote a letter to **George**.

5) **Anita's** house is in the country.

6) "That book is **Katie's**," Katie said.

7) "That is **Laura and Katie's** room," Katie said.

8) "**Katie** is late," Laura said.

9) **Lian and I** are going to the dance.

Activity C   Rewrite each of these sentences on your paper. Replace the words in bold with a pronoun.

Example   At the end of the first day of school, **Gina** was tired.

At the end of the first day of school, **she** was tired.

1) **Gina and Karen** waited for the school bus.

2) "The teacher gave **Gina** homework," Gina said.

3) Gina decided to do **homework** as soon as she got home.

4) **Gina's** homework was not difficult.

5) The teacher told **Gina** to write a paragraph in Spanish.

6) "What is the paragraph about?" **Karen** asked.

7) "What I did on **Gina's** vacation, of course!" Gina laughed.

Activity D Write the pronoun or pronouns in each of these sentences on your paper. Beside each pronoun, write its antecedent.

Example   Finally **Corey and Beth** got on **their** bus.

           their *(personal pronoun)*   **Corey and Beth** *(antecedent)*

1) Jennifer had her Spanish book.

2) She and Michelle talked all the way home.

3) They laughed about a joke Luís had told them.

4) "The kids at school took a vote. They decided Luís tells the best jokes," Jennifer said.

5) "He is a funny person!" Michelle agreed.

6) "I am hungry," Jennifer said.

7) "You can stop by my house," Michelle said. "We can fix a hamburger."

8) "A hamburger sounds very good to me," Jennifer said.

9) "I think your mother left you a note," Jennifer said.

10) Michelle asked, "What does it say?"

11) "She wants you to pick up your brother from day care," Jennifer replied.

12) "We can eat our hamburgers first. Then I will go get him," Michelle said.

- Self pronoun
A pronoun that ends with -self and indicates action done to or by another pronoun or a noun in the sentence. -Self pronouns are also used to show emphasis.

-*Self* **pronouns** refer to another pronoun or a noun. They always come after the noun or pronoun to which they refer. Sometimes -*self* pronouns are used to show emphasis.

EXAMPLES	I hurt **myself**. (indicates action done to the pronoun *I*)
	The child played by **herself**. (indicates action done by the noun *child*)
	Luís ate the whole pie **himself**. (shows emphasis)

Les

Relat
pron

The pr
whom
which
whoev
which
whate

-Self Pronouns		
	Singular	**Plural**
First person	myself	ourselves
Second person	yourself	yourselves
Third person	himself, herself, itself	themselves

Activity E   Write the -*self* pronouns in these sentences on your paper. Beside each -*self* pronoun, write *singular* or *plural*.

Example   Janet studied her math by herself.

   herself—singular

1) The glass fell off the shelf by itself.

2) Ema and Janet cleaned the kitchen themselves.

3) I myself prefer spicy food.

4) We cooked dinner by ourselves.

5) Try to answer the question by yourself.

6) The baby sat up by himself.

7) Clean up this mess by yourselves.

8) He went to the movies by himself.

9) She whispered something to herself.

Activity B The relative pronouns in these sentences are in bold. Write each relative pronoun on your paper. Beside each relative pronoun, write its antecedent.

Example The car **that** Alex bought is blue and white.

that (*relative pronoun*) **car** (*antecedent*)

1) The man **who** owned the garage sold Alex new tires.

2) He is the man **whom** I met last week.

3) Andy likes cars **that** have four-wheel drive.

4) The mechanic has a car **that** is an antique.

5) Did you see the screwdriver **that** I was using?

Activity C Find the relative pronouns in these sentences. Write them on your paper.

1) Do whatever you think should be done.

2) My sister, who wants to be an actress, tried out for the school play.

3) My dog, which is a hound, barks at everyone.

4) You may have whatever you want for dinner.

5) Here are the shoes that I bought.

6) Andy has a friend whose cousin caught a forty-pound fish.

7) Whoever wants to go first should come upstairs now.

8) I found what I wanted.

9) I know the man who won the lottery.

10) Eleni rented the video that you wanted to see.

Activity D   Write the pronouns in the list below on your paper.

1) himself	**8)** bus	**15)** friend
2) whoever	**9)** lady	**16)** you
3) car	**10)** Ms. Woo	**17)** whatever
4) Andy	**11)** I	**18)** themselves
5) which	**12)** what	**19)** its
6) that	**13)** whom	**20)** happiness
7) he	**14)** school	**21)** she

Activity E   Make two columns on your paper. Write *Personal Pronouns* at the top of the first column. Write *Relative Pronouns* at the top of the second column. Then write the pronouns below in the correct column.

1) we	**8)** you	**15)** whom
2) that	**9)** who	**16)** whichever
3) which	**10)** ours	**17)** that
4) what	**11)** them	**18)** themselves
5) mine	**12)** whose	**19)** whoever
6) its	**13)** us	**20)** whatever
7) I	**14)** itself	**21)** he

Activity F   Write the pronoun that should appear in each sentence to make it correct.

1) There are the shoes (who, that) I want.

2) My dog, (who, which) is still a puppy, eats anything.

3) There is the lady (whom, what) I met last week.

4) I like a house (who, that) has a big yard.

Part A   Write the relative pronouns in these sentences on your paper. Include the compound relative pronouns. Beside the pronoun, write its antecedent.

Example   I like food that is very spicy.

that *(relative pronoun)*   **food** *(antecedent)*

1) The mechanic who checked Alex's car did a good job.

2) Alex said to Andy and Frank, "Whoever wants to go for a ride should come now."

3) At the video store, choose whatever you would like to see.

4) There is the man whom I met in Florida.

5) We have steak and chicken. You may have whichever you prefer.

6) Will had a friend whose sister was in the play.

7) Did you see the jeans that I was wearing?

8) Deena has a ring that belonged to her grandmother.

9) I got the gift that I wanted for my birthday.

10) Theo, who is my cousin, works at the mall.

Part B   Write the pronoun that should appear in each sentence to make it correct.

1) (Who, What) is that man?

2) The skateboard (who, that) Hank bought was expensive.

3) I need a chair (who, that) has a high back.

4) My sister, (who, that) is a secretary, just got a raise.

5) Did you see the pen (who, that) I was using?

Pronouns That Ask Questions

Interrogative pronouns

Pronouns that introduce questions: who, whom, which, what, and whose.

An **interrogative pronoun** introduces a question. These pronouns are *who, whom, which, what,* and *whose.*

EXAMPLES

Who is planning the dance?

Whom did you ask to the dance?

Which shoes did Katie buy?

What pages are we to read for homework?

Whose book is on the table?

Who, whom, which, what, and *whose* are interrogative pronouns only when they ask a question.

EXAMPLES

Interrogative: **Who** is going with Andy to the dance?

Relative: Andy asked a girl **who** is in his class.

Activity A   Some pronouns in these sentences are in bold. Write them on your paper. Beside each pronoun, write whether it is *interrogative* or *relative.*

1) **Which** season of the year do you like best?

2) **What** is the name of your book?

3) Tell me the people **who** are going to the dance.

4) Do you know **what** the answer is?

5) **Who** is your favorite singer?

6) **Whom** do you like the most?

7) He is the man **whose** billfold I found.

Interrogative pronouns must agree with their antecedents. The antecedents are the answers to the questions that the interrogative pronouns ask.

Use *who, whom,* or *whose* when the answer to the question is a person or people.

EXAMPLES **Who** is your English teacher?

Whom did you see on the bus?

Whose idea was that?

Use *what* when the answer to the question is a thing, place, or idea.

EXAMPLES **What** is the name of your street?

What are your answers to the first three questions?

Use *which* when the answer to the question is a choice between two or more definite people or things.

EXAMPLES **Which** boy will win the race?

Which newspaper do you read?

Activity B Write the pronoun that should appear in each sentence to make it correct.

1) (Which, What) of these fish is larger?

2) (Which, What) do you want for dinner?

3) (Who, What) will win the World Series?

4) (Who, Whose) mother teaches at our school?

5) (Whom, Whose) did Kevin ask to the dance?

6) (Who, Which) plays third base for the team?

7) (Who, What) is the world's tallest building?

Activity C Make two columns on your paper. Write *Interrogative Pronouns* at the top of the first column. Write *Relative Pronouns* at the top of the second column. Then find the interrogative and relative pronouns in the sentences below. Write them in the correct column.

Example Which of the teams that you played on was the best?

Interrogative Pronouns	*Relative Pronouns*
Which	**that**

1) Alex has a friend whose uncle lives in Canada.

2) Name all of the states that you have visited.

3) What is the name of your book?

4) Choose the book that you want.

5) Tell me which book you like best.

6) Who is the coach of your baseball team?

7) Which tree is taller?

8) What is your favorite subject in school?

9) Do whatever you think is right.

10) Which of the books is the one that the author signed?

Part A   Write the interrogative pronouns in these sentences on your paper.

1) Which ocean do you live closest to, Atlantic or Pacific?

2) Who wrote that book?

3) What country does Queen Elizabeth rule?

4) Whose jacket is on the chair?

5) Whom did you see at the mall?

Part B   Write the pronouns in these sentences on your paper. Beside each pronoun, write whether it is *personal, relative,* or *interrogative.*

Example   What is the movie that you saw yesterday?

What — interrogative

that — relative

you — personal

1) It was Friday night. Alex and Andy talked about what they would like to do.

2) "What is playing at the movies?" Alex asked.

3) "Whatever is playing is okay with me," Andy said.

4) "Which theater should we go to?" Alex asked.

5) "The theater that has the best prices," Andy joked.

6) "Who else might like to go with us?" Alex asked.

7) "I think that I will ask Katie," Andy answered.

8) Alex thought for a moment about which girl he could ask.

9) "What is the name of Katie's friend? Is it Laura? I think that I will ask her," Alex decided.

10) "Whomever you decide to ask, make it quick. The movie starts soon," Andy said.

Demonstrative pronouns

Pronouns that point to nouns: *this, these, that, and those.*

Demonstrative pronouns refer to nouns. *This* and *that* are used with singular nouns. *These* and *those* are used with plural nouns.

EXAMPLES	Singular:	**This** is my book.
	Plural:	**These** are my books.
	Singular:	**That** is an expensive house.
	Plural:	**Those** are expensive houses.

This and *these* point out persons and things that are close. *That* and *those* point out persons and things that are farther away.

EXAMPLES	**This** is my house. **That** is my house.

Activity A Write these sentences on your paper. Circle the demonstrative pronouns.

1) Is that the movie you saw?

2) Those are new socks.

3) These are the pictures from my vacation.

4) Hang that up in the closet, please.

5) This is my neighbor, Mrs. Loomis.

6) Those are beautiful flowers.

7) Are these your favorite colors?

8) This is our neighbor's new puppy.

9) That is my uncle's new car.

10) Is this the book you wanted?

Activity B Write the pronoun that should appear in each sentence to make it correct.

1) Was (this, that) a shooting star I saw?

2) (This, These) is my house.

3) Look across the street. (These, Those) are new houses.

4) Are (that, those) the people who just moved in?

5) "(This, Those) just came for you," Mrs. Thomas said as she handed Kate a big package.

6) (That, Those) is my best friend.

7) Tom bought two new CDs. "(These, That) are really great!" he said to Jamal.

8) A car went speeding down the street. "Did you see (this, that)?" asked Amanda.

9) "I made fruit salad for dessert," said Aunt Tina. "Do you like (that, those)?"

10) "(These, That) are my favorite jeans," Zach said to Marco.

Activity C Write a sentence using each of the demonstrative pronouns.

1) this

2) that

3) these

4) those

Part A   Write the demonstrative pronouns in these sentences on your paper.

1) Do you think Nicole would like these?

2) Those are exactly alike.

3) Pick that up, please.

4) These are very beautiful poems.

5) Is this yours?

6) Did you see that?

7) Tim gave me this.

8) Does that belong to Anna?

9) This is Sal's house.

10) Those are friends of Tyrone.

Part B   Write the pronouns in these sentences on your paper. Beside each pronoun, write whether it is *personal*, *relative*, *interrogative*, or *demonstrative*.

Example   "Who said that?" Michael asked.

Who — interrogative   that — demonstrative

1) Alex works at a store that sells men's clothes.

2) "Which evenings am I working?" he asked.

3) "Whichever you want," said his boss, Mr. Jackson.

4) Alex decided on the hours that he wanted.

5) "What department am I in tonight?" Alex asked.

6) "Go to the stockroom and help them with inventory."

7) Alex asked the people who were in the stockroom what he should do first.

8) "You can start by counting those," said the woman who was in charge.

Indefinite pronoun

A pronoun that refers to a noun that is not named.

Indefinite pronouns replace nouns that are understood by the listener or reader. Some indefinite pronouns are always singular. Some indefinite pronouns are always plural.

These indefinite pronouns are always singular:

another	everybody	nothing
anybody	everyone	one
anyone	everything	one another
anything	much	somebody
each	neither	someone
each other	nobody	something
either	no one	

A singular indefinite pronoun takes a singular verb. Do not get confused by words that come between the subject and verb.

EXAMPLES | Correct: **Everyone has** a ticket.

Neither of us **wants** to miss the beach.

Incorrect: **Neither** of us **want** to miss the beach.

The following indefinite pronouns are always plural:

both	many	several
few	others	

A plural indefinite pronoun takes a plural verb.

EXAMPLES | **Several** of the guests **have** arrived.

The **others are** on their way.

Some indefinite pronouns may be singular or plural, depending on their use. These indefinite pronouns may be singular or plural:

all	most	several
any	none	

When an indefinite pronoun refers to a singular word, the indefinite pronoun is singular. It takes a singular verb.

EXAMPLES **None** of the test **was** hard. (*None* refers to *test,* a singular noun.)

All of the garden **looks** beautiful. (*All* refers to *garden*, a singular noun.)

When an indefinite pronoun refers to a plural word, the indefinite pronoun is plural. It takes a plural verb.

EXAMPLES **None** of the questions **were** hard. (*None* refers to *questions*, a plural noun.)

All of the flowers **look** beautiful. (*All* refers to *flowers,* a plural noun.)

When an indefinite pronoun is the antecedent of another pronoun, be sure that both pronouns agree in number.

EXAMPLES **All** of the boys took **their** seats. (*All* is plural and is the antecedent of *their*.)

Every **one** of the girls has **her** ticket. (*One* is singular and is the antecedent of *her*.)

If the gender of the indefinite pronoun is not clear, you may use both the masculine and feminine pronouns.

EXAMPLE **Everyone** brought **his** or **her** ticket.

Activity A   Write the indefinite pronouns in these sentences on your paper.

1) Everyone brought food to the picnic.

2) Jack did not know anyone at the party.

3) None of the boys were late.

4) Try to be nice to one another.

5) Few of the students enjoyed the bus ride.

6) Everyone talked to the bride at the wedding.

7) Each of the guests brought a present.

8) Sam saw no one that he knew.

9) Li knew some of the people in the class.

10) Everything is ready for the party.

11) Try to help each other.

12) Some of the food was too spicy.

13) Karl knew nothing about the Red River.

14) Julia knows someone in that neighborhood.

15) Other than Sara, I do not know anyone here.

Activity B   Write the word that should appear in each sentence to make it correct.

1) Everybody (is, are) coming to the party.

2) Everything in the closet (is, are) Katie's.

3) Some of those people (is, are) going home now.

4) Someone (is, are) reading that book.

5) Somebody (has, have) my pencil.

6) Everyone must leave (his or her, their) coat on.

7) Several of the guests (was, were) late.

8) Each of the men brought (his, their) wife.

9) None of the children remembered (his or her, their) lunch.

10) One of those coats is missing (its, their) buttons.

Part A   Write a sentence on your paper for each of these indefinite pronouns.

1) someone

2) everyone

3) no one

4) anybody

5) nothing

6) none

7) everything

8) something

9) all

10) nobody

Part B   Find ten indefinite pronouns in these sentences. Write them on your paper.

1) Everyone in Mr. Jackson's store was getting ready for the fall sale.

2) All of the salespeople came to work early that day.

3) Everybody was quiet as he or she worked.

4) Nobody said anything.

5) Suddenly someone laughed.

6) "Why are we all so quiet?" one of the women asked.

7) They all looked at each other.

8) "Some of us remember last year's sale," Alex said.

9) "I think many of you will need a vacation after today," he said.

Part A Write the pronouns in these sentences on your paper.

1) Katie looked for her new homeroom.

2) She walked up the stairs to the third floor.

3) Katie found an old friend. They were in the same homeroom.

4) "This must be the place," said Katie.

5) "Lucky us!" laughed Laura.

Part B The pronouns in these sentences are in bold. Write the pronouns on your paper. Beside each pronoun, write whether it is *personal*, *relative*, *interrogative*, *demonstrative*, or *indefinite*.

Example **That** is the **one that** I like best.

That—demonstrative   that—relative

one—indefinite   I—personal

1) **It** was the dry season of the year.

2) **Everyone** was watering **his** or **her** yard.

3) **No one** was expecting rain for a while.

4) "**Everybody** must try to save water," Mr. Jones announced.

5) "**What** should **we** do?" **one** of the neighbors asked.

6) "**We** could stop watering **our** lawns," **someone** said.

7) "**I** suggest **that each** of **us** water only once a week," Mrs. Mendez said.

8) "**That** is a good idea," Katie said, and **all** of the neighbors agreed.

9) "The people on the even side of the street should water on weekdays," **she** said.

10) **Those who** live on the odd side will water on weekends.

Part C Write the word that should appear in each sentence to make it correct.

1) Chris was a person (who, which) liked to be active.

2) "I think I need more exercise," he told (hisself, himself).

3) "(Whose, What) type of exercise would I enjoy the most?"

4) "Biking is an exercise (whom, that) I would enjoy."

5) He heard of a new bike trail in the next town. "(This, That) would be a good place to go," he said.

6) "(Which, Who) of my friends might like to join me?"

7) "Rico is someone (whom, which) I could ask."

8) "Nobody (enjoy, enjoys) the outdoors as much as Rico."

9) "We must wear helmets to protect (ourself, ourselves)," Rico said.

10) "Is (this, that) the safest helmet in the store?" Chris asked, pointing to the helmet on the top shelf.

11) "(Whose, Which) do you think I should buy?" he asked Rico.

12) "Either of those (is, are) fine."

13) "I think my bike is missing one of (its, it's) parts," Rico said.

14) "Do (whatever, whichever) needs to be done to get ready for our ride," Chris said.

15) "This is going to be great," both of the boys agreed as they began (his, their) ride.

Test Taking Tip Be sure you understand what the test question is asking. Reread it if you have to.

Chapter 3

The Adjective

When you tell someone about something you have seen, you use words to help the person picture what you saw. When you tell someone about something you have heard, you use words to help the person imagine the sounds you heard.

An adjective is a word that describes a noun or a pronoun. You make your ideas clearer and more interesting by using adjectives.

In Chapter 3, you will learn about adjectives. Each lesson in the chapter focuses on a different type of adjective and its use in writing and speaking.

Goals for Learning

▶ To recognize adjectives in sentences and to identify the nouns that the adjectives describe

▶ To recognize articles and numbers used as adjectives in sentences

▶ To recognize and capitalize proper adjectives

▶ To recognize demonstrative pronouns and possessive nouns used as adjectives

▶ To use adjectives correctly to make comparisons

53

Adjective

A word that tells about a noun or a pronoun. An adjective tells what kind, which one, how many, or how much.

An **adjective** is a word that describes a noun or pronoun. An adjective answers the question *What kind? Which one? How many?* or *How much?* about a noun or a pronoun. More than one adjective may be used to describe a noun or a pronoun.

 EXAMPLES

What kind?	We stayed in a **small beach** house.
Which one?	I live in **that** house.
How many?	We have lived in **five** states.
How much?	He had **some** money.

Activity A   Some of the adjectives in these sentences are in bold. Write the adjectives on your paper. Next to the adjective, write the noun that the adjective describes.

Example   David bought an **expensive new** reel.

   expensive new—reel

1) What a **fantastic summer** vacation they had at the lake!

2) We did not have **enough** time to do everything.

3) On the **first** day we were there, Vince caught a **huge** fish.

4) The **next** day, David hooked **three** trout.

5) At night, a **big black** bear came into **our** camp.

Activity B   Rewrite these sentences on your paper. Add one or more adjectives before each noun in bold.

1) Students brought **books** to **class**.

2) **People** brought **food**.

3) **School** started early.

4) I saw **mountains** and **rivers**.

5) Diana planted **tomatoes** and **cucumbers**.

Most adjectives come before the noun that they are describing. Adjectives may, however, follow the noun for emphasis. Then, they are set off from the rest of the sentence with commas.

> **EXAMPLES** The **sleepy** child was crying.
>
> The child, **sleepy** and **hungry**, was crying.

A **predicate adjective** comes after the noun or pronoun it describes.

> **EXAMPLES** He was **sleepy** and **hungry**.
>
> They seem **happy**.

Activity C   Find the adjectives in these sentences. Write them on your paper. Beside each adjective, write the noun or pronoun that the adjective describes.

1) The lake was beautiful on that morning.
2) The water was clear and cool.
3) David saw a large fish jump out of the sparkling water.
4) Vince used a trusty old rod.
5) The boys fished for eight hours.
6) For a long time, nothing happened.
7) They remained hopeful.
8) By late afternoon, they had caught many fish.
9) They were tired but happy with themselves.
10) Vince told funny stories as they rode home.

Part A   Some of the adjectives in these sentences are in bold. Write them on your paper. Beside each one, write the noun or pronoun that the adjective describes.

1) In October, the weather can be **chilly**.

2) David decided to wear a **heavy** coat.

3) He had **several** classes on Wednesdays.

4) David's **favorite** class was math.

5) Math was **easy** for him.

6) He drove to the college in **his** car.

Part B   Rewrite these sentences on your paper. Add as many adjectives as you can to each sentence. Circle all the adjectives in your sentences.

1) Diana has a dog.

2) David bought a coat.

3) The fisher cast a line into the lake.

4) It was morning.

5) The store had a sale.

6) I have a job.

7) Ray plays piano.

8) Annie's jacket has a hole in it.

The articles *a, an,* and *the* are always used as adjectives. They are placed before nouns in sentences. The definite article is *the.* Use *the* when you are talking about a particular person or thing. The indefinite articles are *a* and *an.* Use *a* or *an* when you are talking about a general group of people or things.

EXAMPLES	
	Sharon wanted to go to **a** movie. (Sharon does not have a particular movie in mind.)
	Vince would like to see **an** adventure movie. (Vince wants to see any adventure movie.)
	Eli saw **the** movie yesterday. (Eli saw a particular movie.)

Use the article *a* before a word that begins with a consonant sound. Use the article *an* before a word that begins with a vowel sound.

EXAMPLES		
	a large apple	an apple
	a hard assignment	an assignment
	a mistake	an honest mistake

The article *a* is used with singular nouns. The article *the* can be used with singular and plural nouns.

EXAMPLES	
	I bought **a** book. (*Book* is singular.)
	David bought **the** book. (*Book* is singular.)
	He bought **the** books. (*Books* is plural.)

Activity A Write these sentences on your paper. Circle all of the articles.

1) The math class was the first class of the day.

2) The students had a homework assignment.

3) The first part of the class was easy.

4) The class discussed the answers to the problems.

5) "I got a different answer to the problem," Jamal said.

6) The teacher explained the problem.

7) She used an overhead projector.

8) Later she handed out a new assignment.

Activity B Write the article that should appear in each sentence to make it correct.

1) Suki packed (a, an) apple for her lunch.

2) They waited for (a, an) hour.

3) The teacher spoke in (a, an) soft voice.

4) They had (a, an) English lesson.

5) I read (a, an) article about elephants.

6) He had (a, an) message for his boss.

7) Look up the topic in (a, an) index.

8) They saw (a, an) horror movie.

9) Not (a, an) cloud was in sight.

10) Jack is (a, an) honest man.

Lesson Review Write the article that should appear in each sentence to make it correct.

1) Look at (a, the) blue coat in the window.

2) Did you enjoy eating (a, the) peaches?

3) Mrs. Jones put (a, the) groceries on the table.

4) We went to New York City to see (a, an) play.

5) Chicago is (a, an) American city.

6) They did (a, the) activity in class.

7) A hammer is (a, an) useful tool.

8) Did you see (a, the) pencils I left here?

9) Where is (a, an) envelope?

10) I was in (a, an) earthquake in California.

11) We have (a, an) eight-foot tree in our yard.

12) Have you ever seen (a, an) bald eagle?

13) (A, The) snakes crawled on a rock to sun themselves.

14) They did (a, an) math activity.

15) "What (a, an) awful day this has been!" she said.

16) What happened to (a, the) flower vase?

Adjectives That Are Capitalized

Proper adjectives are made from proper nouns. A proper adjective always begins with a capital letter.

EXAMPLES

Proper noun:	He is an **American**.
Proper adjective:	He is an **American** soldier.
Proper noun:	I visited **Mexico**.
Proper adjective:	I love **Mexican** food.

Activity A Write the proper adjectives in these sentences on your paper. Beside each proper adjective, write the noun or pronoun it describes. Read carefully. Some capitalized words are proper nouns.

1) Bess studied Spanish first period.

2) She almost forgot her Spanish book.

3) In her English class, Bess was studying Shakespearean literature.

4) She liked American literature better.

5) This year in social studies, we learned about Native American cultures.

6) This beautiful woven blanket is Native American.

7) Bess had never tasted Thai food.

Activity B Use these proper adjectives in sentences. Write the sentences on your paper. Be sure to use these words as adjectives that describe nouns or pronouns.

1) Spanish

2) German

3) Chinese

4) Democratic

5) African

6) Brazilian

7) American

8) Olympic

Activity C Complete each sentence with a proper adjective. Write the complete sentence on your paper.

1) We ordered _____ dressing for our salad.

2) Mr. Cruz likes _____ cheese.

3) Lori studied the _____ language last year.

4) They live in Germany, but they are _____ citizens.

5) He belongs to the _____ political party.

6) Is _____ cooking easier than it looks?

7) We saw examples of _____ art.

8) Both his grandparents are _____.

Activity D Write the words in bold on your paper. Beside each word, write whether it is used as a proper noun or a proper adjective. Beside each proper adjective, write the noun or pronoun it describes.

1) I like **French** onion soup.

2) Mark lives in **Philadelphia**.

3) He is a **Philadelphia** boy.

4) Kareem watched the **Russian** jugglers.

5) He practiced saying "hello" and "good-bye" in **Russian**.

6) Amy Tan is an **Asian American** writer.

7) Next summer I want to travel along the **Spanish** coast.

8) I'd like to study **Spanish** first.

9) The exchange student who stayed with us last year was **Spanish**.

10) The instructions for the VCR were in **Japanese**.

11) The high school band will march in the **Thanksgiving Day** parade.

12) That is an **African** elephant.

Part A Write these sentences on your paper. Capitalize all of the proper adjectives. Then draw an arrow from the proper adjective to the noun it describes.

Example Jon likes the beat of Latin music.

1) My older sister fixed up that old ford truck.

2) He likes swiss cheese.

3) We read several spanish and italian folktales.

4) They spent the summer camping along the maine coast.

5) Melissa's father is american and her mother is canadian.

6) You are invited to our memorial day picnic.

Part B Make each proper noun a proper adjective and use it in a sentence. Write the sentences on your paper. Draw an arrow from each proper adjective to the noun or pronoun it describes.

1) Germany

2) Fourth of July

3) Spain

4) United States

5) Democrat

6) South America

7) China

Common nouns can be used as adjectives. To figure out if a word is a noun or an adjective, look at how it is used in the sentence.

EXAMPLES

Noun:	Paul ordered a large **salad**.
Adjective:	What kind of **salad** dressing would you like? (*Salad* describes the noun *dressing*.)
Noun:	Vera plays **basketball**.
Adjective:	Vera plays on the **basketball** team. (*Basketball* describes the noun *team*.)

Activity A   Write the words in bold on your paper. Beside each word, write whether it is a *noun* or an *adjective*. If a word is an adjective, write the noun that the adjective describes.

1) I'm looking for a **summer** job.

2) My sister found a great job for the **summer**.

3) She was hired by the **city**.

4) It sponsors a **jobs** program for teens.

5) Vera will be working as a **park** leader.

6) She will probably work at the **park** near our house.

7) The pay is good for a **city** job.

8) She gets to be outside all day playing **basketball** with little kids.

9) Wasn't Vera one of the best **basketball** players on the girls' team?

10) In fact, three different **college** coaches have called her.

11) They have offered her a **scholarship** to play at their school.

12) Vera has not decided which **college** she will go to yet.

Part A Write the common nouns used as adjectives in these sentences on your paper. Beside each adjective, write the noun it describes.

1) Bill grabbed his lunch bag and ran out the door.

2) He was going to be late for the newspaper meeting.

3) Bill enjoyed working on the school paper.

4) As the sports reporter, he went to all the games.

5) Talking to team members before and after the games was fun.

6) Last week, he covered a big track event.

7) The night before, he joined the team for a spaghetti dinner.

8) On the bus ride the next day, he spoke to the coaches and athletes.

9) He jotted down his interview notes in a notebook.

10) After the game, he went to the computer room at school to write his article.

Part B Write a sentence on your paper using each of these common nouns as an adjective. Draw an arrow from the adjective to the noun it describes.

1) baseball

2) fruit

3) winter

4) tomato

5) school

Possessive pronouns are sometimes called possessive adjectives. They tell something about the nouns they describe. A possessive adjective describes a noun by telling which one or whose.

> **EXAMPLES**   **His** house is on the corner. (Which house? *his* house)
> Is that **their** room? (Whose room? *their* room)

A possessive adjective can be used with a possessive noun.

> **EXAMPLE**   That is **my sister's** book.
> (The possessive adjective *my* describes *sister*.
> Whose sister? *my* sister)
> (The possessive noun *sister's* shows ownership.
> Whose book? *sister's* book)

Activity A   The possessive adjectives in these sentences are in bold. Write them on your paper. Beside each possessive adjective, write the noun it describes.

Example   He left **his** hat on the bus.
        his — hat

1) I always like to get **my** money's worth.
2) **Our** family has always shopped in **their** store.
3) **Your** dog has a guilty look on **its** face.
4) We are having **her** birthday party next Saturday.
5) **His** picture was in the newspaper yesterday.

Activity B   Find the possessive adjectives in these sentences. Write them on your paper. Beside each possessive adjective, write the noun it describes.

1) His bike is missing.
2) Your coat was in the living room.
3) I helped my mother's friend look for her ring.
4) There was a rabbit in my garden.
5) Their dog likes to hide its bones under our porch.

Lesson Review   Find the possessive adjectives in these sentences. List them on your paper in order. Beside each one, write the noun that the adjective describes.

1) Dave and Vince did their math homework together.

2) "Your second answer is wrong," Dave said.

3) "Here is my answer."

4) Dave tried to explain his answer.

5) "I think both of our answers are wrong," Vince said.

6) They compared their problems.

7) "We should check our math," Vince suggested.

8) "Use my calculator to check."

9) The calculator did not work because its battery was dead.

10) Vince found some new batteries in his desk.

A number can be used as an adjective to describe a noun. Numbers describe by telling how many.

EXAMPLES   Mrs. Jones canned **twenty** jars of pears.
(How many jars? *twenty*)

Twelve people came to the party.
(How many people? *twelve*)

An indefinite pronoun also can be used as an adjective to describe a noun. When indefinite pronouns are used as adjectives, they describe by telling how many. However, the amount is not exact.

EXAMPLES   Pronoun: **Several** of the guests arrived late.

Adjective: **Several** years went by before I saw her again. (How many years? *several*)

Activity A   Write a sentence on your paper for each number word listed below. Use the word as an adjective. Circle the noun or pronoun that the adjective describes.

1) few	**4)** some	**7)** four
2) thirty-three	**5)** most	**8)** several
3) one	**6)** eighty	**9)** all

Activity B   The number words used as adjectives in the following sentences are in bold. Write them on your paper. Beside each adjective, write the noun that the adjective describes.

Example   **Many** people read that book.
           Many — people

1) **Twenty-five** people signed up for the class.

2) **One** student dropped out.

3) After a **few** weeks, the teacher gave a test.

4) **Several** members of the class got a perfect grade.

5) **Most** students enjoyed the class.

Activity C The number words in these sentences are in bold. Write them on your paper. Beside each one, write whether it is used as a *pronoun* or an *adjective*.

Example **All** of the students signed up for **six** classes.

          All—pronoun

          six—adjective

1) The hurricane winds were **eighty** miles an hour.

2) The storm lasted for **several** hours.

3) **Everyone** on the block watched the storm.

4) **Many** trees blew down in the neighborhood.

5) We watched as a **few** cars drove through the storm.

6) **Most** people stayed inside.

7) The electricity was out for **six** hours.

8) **No one** could cook dinner or watch television.

9) **Some** families went out for dinner.

10) **Others** tried to barbecue in their yards.

Part A Write the number words used as adjectives in these sentences on your paper. Beside each adjective, write the noun it describes.

1) One Sunday, several friends and I visited the City Animal Park.

2) Each animal was in a natural setting.

3) We watched three chimpanzees swing from trees.

4) Eight lions and six tigers climbed over a rocky ledge.

5) There were many birds flying around the park.

6) For lunch, Willy ate two tacos and drank some lemonade.

7) We walked around for several hours.

8) Few people wanted to go home.

9) I took twenty-four photographs of the alligators and crocodiles.

10) Most children and adults would enjoy a visit to the City Animal Park.

Part B Complete these sentences by adding a number used as an adjective. Write the complete sentences on your paper.

1) During the hurricane, winds were blowing at _____ miles an hour.

2) _____ friends on our block are going on a picnic today.

3) Derek is taking _____ classes this year.

4) The movie lasted for _____ minutes.

5) _____ people were unhappy about the decision.

The demonstrative pronouns—*this, that, these,* and *those*—can be used as adjectives to describe a noun. They answer the question *Which one or ones?*

EXAMPLES	Pronoun:	**That** is a mistake.
	Adjective:	**That** mistake was Cal's. (Which mistake? *that* one)

Activity A   The demonstratives in these sentences are in bold. Write them on your paper. Beside each one, write whether it is an *adjective* or a *pronoun*.

1) "**This** Sunday, let's go to the football game together," Leslie said.

2) My brother gave me **these** tickets.

3) "Do you think **that** team will win a game **this** year?" Elvin asked.

4) "Some of **those** new players are great," Leslie answered.

5) "I like **that** new fullback."

6) "**This** should be a good season," Elvin said.

7) "**That** will have to be proved," said Leslie.

Activity B   Write these sentences on your paper. Underline five demonstrative adjectives. Then draw an arrow to the noun each demonstrative adjective describes.

Example   Those players are on our team.

1) The football game that day was exciting.

2) "Where are those snacks you promised?"

3) "Look in that cabinet over the refrigerator."

4) "That is where my mother keeps those things."

5) "These sandwiches look good enough to eat."

Lesson Review Find the demonstratives used as adjectives in the following sentences. Write them on your paper. Beside each one, write the noun it describes.

1) On that day, we went to a baseball game.

2) Those people behind us yelled through the whole game.

3) I would have liked to see that last play again.

4) We could have watched this game on television at home.

5) That would not have been as much fun as this day has been.

6) I felt bad for those umpires when the fans booed them.

7) Would you like to keep these ticket stubs to remember the fun we had?

8) Do you think that friend of yours could get us tickets to the next home game?

9) I want to keep these plastic cups from our soft drinks.

10) My sister has a set of those cups.

Positive adjective

An adjective that describes one noun.

Comparative adjective

An adjective that compares one noun with another.

Superlative adjective

An adjective that compares one noun with two or more other nouns.

Adjectives can be used to compare people or things. There are three degrees of comparison: **positive**, **comparative**, and **superlative**.

EXAMPLES	Positive	Comparative	Superlative
	strong	stronger	strongest
	easy	easier	easiest
	big	bigger	biggest
	careful	more careful	most careful
	popular	less popular	least popular
	good	better	best
	bad	worse	worst

Use the positive degree to describe one thing.

Use the comparative degree to compare two things.

Use the superlative degree to compare more than two things.

EXAMPLES

Incorrect: Luke is Darlene's brother. Luke is **oldest**.

Correct: Luke is Darlene's brother. Luke is **older**.
(Two people are being compared.)

Correct: Of the three children, Matt is **oldest**.
(More than two people are being compared.)

Most one-syllable adjectives form their comparative and superlative degrees by adding *-er* and *-est*.

Activity A   Write the adjectives on your paper. Write their comparative and superlative degrees beside each one.

Example   tall — **taller, tallest**

1) young   **4)** short   **7)** late

2) old   **5)** green   **8)** strict

3) kind   **6)** slow   **9)** bright

Some two-syllable adjectives form their comparative and superlative degrees by adding -er and -est. Others form their comparative and superlative degrees by using *more* and *most*.

Positive	Comparative	Superlative
happy	happier	happiest
careful	more careful	most careful

Adjectives of more than two syllables form their comparative and superlative degrees by using *more* and *most*. Adjectives can also be compared with *less* and *least*.

Positive	Comparative	Superlative
wonderful	more wonderful	most wonderful
successful	more successful	most successful
excited	less excited	least excited
generous	less generous	least generous

Activity B   The adjectives in the following sentences are in bold. Write them on your paper. Beside each one, write whether it is *positive, comparative,* or *superlative*.

Example   Danny is the **most helpful** person I know.

   most helpful—superlative

1) That is the **least comfortable** chair.

2) Chris thought the movie was **terrible**.

3) The young girl was the **most talented** actress in the play.

4) I have never seen a **sadder** face.

5) This coat is **less expensive** than the other one.

Some adjectives form their comparative and superlative degrees in an irregular way.

EXAMPLES		
Positive	**Comparative**	**Superlative**
good	better	best
bad	worse	worst

Activity C   Use these adjectives correctly in a sentence. Write the sentences on your paper.

1) least useful

2) smaller

3) most successful

4) more wonderful

5) less careful

6) better

7) worst

8) heaviest

9) lighter

10) best

Activity D   Write the form of the adjective that should appear in each sentence to make it correct.

1) That is the (redder, reddest) sunset I have ever seen.

2) Which of those two buildings is (taller, tallest)?

3) St. Augustine is the (oldest, older) city in Florida.

4) This chair is the (more comfortable, most comfortable) of the two.

5) That movie was the (goodest, best) I have ever seen.

6) Yesterday's homework was (easier, easiest) than today's.

7) Roger is the (least, less) selfish person I know.

8) Kerry is (gracefuller, more graceful) than I could ever be.

Part A Make three columns on your paper as shown in the example. Write the adjectives below in the correct column.

Example *Positive*	*Comparative*	*Superlative*
pretty	**friendlier**	**best**

1) bad

2) prettier

3) less difficult

4) worse

5) more careful

6) easiest

7) less comfortable

8) most generous

9) least horrible

10) worst

11) popular

12) good

Part B Some of the adjectives in these sentences are in bold. Write them on your paper. Beside each one, write whether it is *positive, comparative,* or *superlative.*

1) Emma is **older** than Britt.

2) This cloth feels **nice**, but that one feels **nicer**.

3) Of the two athletes, Lewis is the **faster** runner.

4) That comic is **funny**.

5) Hector plays tennis **better** than his twin brother Paco.

6) Of all the photographs, this one is the **best**.

7) I thought that her voice was soft, but yours is even **softer**.

Part C Write these adjectives on your paper. Beside each one, write its comparative and superlative forms.

1) small

2) useful

3) fast

4) famous

5) stern

6) soft

7) comfortable

8) smart

9) angry

10) horrible

Part A   Write all the adjectives in these sentences on your paper. Be sure to include articles.

1) The day was cool and clear.

2) Everyone was happy about the beautiful autumn weather.

3) After school, Rita and Pat went for a long walk.

4) The weather, sunny and warm, was delightful.

5) A group of young children, noisy but cheerful, got on the bus.

Part B   Write the bold adjectives in these sentences on your paper. Beside each adjective, write the noun or pronoun that the adjective describes.

Example   The **new** car was **expensive**.

        new—car   **expensive—car**

1) The students in **my** homeroom had a meeting.

2) They elected **new** officers for the **school** year.

3) "Li is **smart**, **loyal**, and **fun**," said Sue Ann.

4) "She will be a **good** president."

5) The election was **close**, but Li won.

Part C Write all the adjectives in these sentences on your paper. Be sure to include articles.

1) Joel and Paula decided to have an autumn party.

2) The party was on a Saturday evening.

3) Their parents gave them permission.

4) Paula found some old party decorations in the attic.

5) They bought fifty red apples and ten gallons of cider.

6) Joel carved an enormous pumpkin.

7) Some guests said they should all dunk for the apples.

8) "What an old-fashioned idea!" Paula said.

9) Several people brought more food.

10) Later everyone agreed that the party was the best one yet.

Part D Write the words in bold in these sentences on your paper. Beside each word, write whether it is a *noun* or an *adjective.*

1) That **history** book belongs to James Melcher.

2) They all went to the **meeting** room.

3) The **meeting** began at three o'clock.

4) The **south** wind was warm.

5) The wind came from the **South**.

Test Taking Tip Before you begin a test, look it over quickly. Try to set aside enough time to complete each section.

Chapter 4

The Action Verb

A t home, in the workplace, and in the community, you are often busy moving about and doing things. Exercising, working, eating, and thinking are just a few examples of the actions you do every day. When you talk or write about what you have done or seen, you use words that show action.

A verb is a word that expresses action or a state of being. An action verb is a word that expresses either physical or mental action.

In Chapter 4, you will learn about action verbs. Each lesson in the chapter focuses on the correct use and form of action verbs in sentences.

Goals for Learning

▶ To identify verbs and verb phrases in sentences

▶ To identify the correct form of verbs in sentences

▶ To recognize active and passive verbs

Lesson 1 — Finding the Verb in a Sentence

Action verb

A word that expresses physical or mental action in the past, present, or future.

An **action verb** is a word that expresses the action in a sentence. The verb tells what someone or something does, did, or will do. Find the verb in a sentence by asking yourself two questions:

1. Who or what is doing something? (subject)

2. What are they doing? (verb)

> **EXAMPLE**   Every morning, Mr. Okada **reads** the newspaper.
>
> Who is doing something? *Mr. Okada* (subject)
>
> What does he do? *reads* (verb)

A sentence can have more than one verb.

> **EXAMPLE**   Donna **washed** and **wiped** the dishes after breakfast.
>
> She **opened** her book and **began** her homework.

Some verbs express mental action, which cannot be seen.

> **EXAMPLE**   Mr. Okada **likes** his job.
>
> Donna **thinks** about her test.

Activity A   Write the verbs in these sentences on your paper.

1) Mr. Okada parked his car.

2) Several of his friends waved to him.

3) He likes all the people at the office.

4) Pam called her boss.

5) She reminded him about the meeting.

Activity B   List the subjects and verbs in these sentences. Write *S* beside the subject and *V* beside the verb.

Example   The secretary answers the telephone.

secretary—S   answers—V

1) In the office everyone works hard.

2) Some people sort mail.

3) Others load it on trucks.

4) The trucks haul the mail to other places.

5) Letter carriers deliver mail to homes and offices.

6) Mrs. Davis works in an office.

7) She prepares the payroll.

8) Her assistant enters the information into a computer.

9) The computer prints the checks.

Activity C   Find the verb or verbs in each sentence. List them on your own paper.

Examples   The employees went to their desks and worked.

went, worked

1) Mr. Torres rode his bike to work on Tuesday.

2) He drank some juice and ate a bagel.

3) The telephone rang three times and then stopped.

4) His boss called back a few minutes later.

5) Mr. Torres wondered about the new client, Ms. Peters.

6) He sat in the meeting room and waited for everyone.

7) Ms. Peters and her assistant arrived on time.

8) They all shook hands and said, "Hello."

Verb phrase

A main verb and one
or more helping verbs.

A **verb phrase** is made up of more than one verb. A verb phrase contains a main verb and one or more helping verbs. The helping verbs *help* the main verb to show action.

EXAMPLES   Mr. Torres **has poured** his juice.

poured—main verb   *has*—helping verb

Annie **should have come** with us.

come—main verb   *should have*—helping verbs

Activity D   Write the verb or verb phrase in each of these sentences on your paper.

1) Mrs. Stamos had spoken to Mr. Franklin.

2) Later, he thought about their talk.

3) He should have known about the problem sooner.

4) They could have helped each other.

5) Mr. Franklin has announced a new policy.

6) From now on, workers will meet with their supervisors once a week.

7) All of the employees support the new policy.

Activity E   Use each verb or verb phrase below in a sentence. Write the sentences on your paper. Underline each subject once and each verb or verb phrase twice.

1) accept

2) balance

3) will comfort

4) contain

5) lift

6) could have been

7) examine

8) write

9) should remember

10) may think

Part A   Write the verbs in these sentences on your paper.

1) Many different people work at the post office.
2) The public appreciates their efforts.
3) Letters and packages stream into the post office all day and night.
4) Letter carriers load the mail into sacks and deliver it.
5) Mail comes to the post office on trucks.
6) Airplanes also carry mail across the country and the world.
7) Millions of pieces of mail travel from place to place.
8) At the post office, mail handlers unload mail.
9) In smaller post offices, the workers sort the mail.
10) Machines perform this job in big cities.

Part B   Write the verb or verb phrase in each of these sentences on your paper.

Example   Don has gone to the store.

has gone

1) The newspaper arrived at six o'clock every day.
2) Mrs. Turner heard a thud at the front door.
3) She opened the door.
4) Then she got the paper.
5) She carried it into the kitchen.
6) Mr. Turner scrambled the eggs and put bread into the toaster.
7) He smiled at his wife.
8) She had set the table and had poured their juice.
9) They sat and read the paper.
10) Mr. and Mrs. Turner started every day the same way.
11) By six-thirty, they had eaten and had washed the dishes.
12) Then they both left for work.
13) He took the bus to his job downtown.
14) She drove the car to her office.
15) Each of them looks forward to the weekend.

Tense

The time that the verb expresses in a sentence.

The verb in a sentence expresses **tense**, or time. Verbs use endings, helping verbs, or both to express tense.

Every verb has an infinitive form which is *to* plus the present tense of the verb. Verbs can express present, past, and future tense. Form the past tense by adding *-ed* to the present tense. Form the future tense by using the helping verb *will* or *shall*.

EXAMPLES

Infinitive: **to fish**

Present tense: I **fish** in that lake all summer.
(Shows an action done in the present time.)

Past tense: I **fished** in that lake last summer.
(Shows an action done in the past.)

Future tense: I **will fish** in that lake next summer.
(Shows an action that will be done in the future.)

Activity A   The verb in each of these sentences is in bold. Write the tense of the verb on your paper.

1) The Wilson Wildcats **will play** their first football game on Saturday.

2) The team **practices** every day.

3) They **wondered** about their opponents.

4) The coach **called** the team together.

5) He **talked** to them about the game plan.

6) "I **believe** in you guys."

7) The team **knows** the plan.

8) They **want** a victory on Saturday.

9) They **will do** their very best.

Add -*s* or -*es* to the present tense of the verb if the subject is singular.

> **EXAMPLES**   Singular subject: James **practices** every day.
>
> Plural subject: The players **practice** every day.

Remember: collective nouns (names of groups acting as one) are singular. Some indefinite pronouns, such as *everyone*, are also singular.

> **EXAMPLES**
>
> Singular subject: The team **practices** after school.
>
> Plural subject: Both teams **practice** after school.
>
> Singular subject: Everyone **wants** a victory.

Activity B   Write the verb that should appear in each sentence to make it correct.

1) James (hope, hopes) for a victory.

2) He (play, plays) tackle on the team.

3) Greg and Lorenzo both (play, plays) quarterback.

4) The coach (choose, chooses) the quarterback for each game.

5) Adam (catch, catches) every pass during practice.

6) All of them (go, goes) to practice every day.

7) Everyone (look, looks) forward to the games.

8) The whole team (work, works) hard.

Present perfect

The verb tense that shows an action started in the past and continuing up to the present.

The three perfect tenses are **present perfect**, **past perfect**, and **future perfect**. They are formed by using the helping verb *have*.

EXAMPLES

Present perfect:	James **has tackled** his opponent many times.
	(Shows an action that started in the past and continues up to the present. This action is likely to happen again.)

Past perfect

The verb tense that shows one action completed before another past action.

Past perfect:	James **had tackled** him before the whistle blew.
	(Shows that one action was completed before another past action began.)

Future perfect

The verb tense that shows an action that will be completed before a certain time in the future.

Future perfect:	In a few minutes, our team **will have won** the game.
	(Shows an action that will be completed before a certain time in the future.)

Regular verbs form their past tense by adding *-ed* to the present tense. Irregular verbs form their past tense in different ways. *Have* is an irregular verb.

You need to know the different forms of *have* to form the perfect tenses of verbs.

(To) Have		
Present tense	(singular)	James **has** the football now.
	(plural)	They **have** nine points.
Past tense		The team **had** the lead.
Future tense		The team **will have** a victory.
Present perfect	(singular)	He **has had** the ball three times.
	(plural)	They **have had** the ball most of the game.
Past perfect		When the quarter ended, they **had had** enough.
Future perfect		In one week, we **shall have had** a winning season.

The verb *have* can be a main verb or a helping verb.

Have as a main verb:	I **have** a good team.
	(*have* used alone)
Have as a helping verb:	I **have scored** a touchdown.
	(*have* used with the verb *scored*)

Activity C   Write the verb that should appear in each sentence to make it correct.

1) The Wilson Wildcats (has, have) the football.

2) The team (has, have) scored a touchdown.

3) The Wildcats have (have, had) the ball for most of the quarter.

4) They will (has, have) given the other team few chances.

5) We soon will (have, had) earned the victory.

Activity D   Decide whether *have* is the main verb or the helping verb in each sentence. Write your answers on your paper.

1) The quarterback has worked hard today.

2) He has thrown several good passes.

3) Hector has a good record so far.

4) We have one win and no losses.

5) The coach has expressed high hopes for the rest of the season.

Activity E   Write the present perfect, past perfect, and future perfect tenses of the verbs below in sentences on your paper. Underline the verb in each sentence.

Example   jump

He <u>has jumped</u>. He <u>had jumped</u>. He <u>will have jumped</u>.

1) act

6) offer

2) discuss

7) open

3) improve

8) pass

4) lock

9) yell

5) move

10) shout

Activity F   Write all six tenses of the verbs below in sentences on your paper. Use the third person singular (he, she, or it). Underline the verb in each sentence.

Example   whisper

present: She <u>whispers</u>.

past: She <u>whispered</u>.

future: She <u>will whisper</u>.

present perfect: She <u>has whispered</u>.

past perfect: She <u>had whispered</u>.

future perfect: She <u>will have whispered</u>.

1) walk

2) work

3) fish

4) listen

5) roar

Remember: Most verbs in the English language are regular. They form their past and perfect tenses by adding *-d* or *-ed* to their present form.

When a verb ends in *-y* and the letter before the *-y* is a consonant, change the *-y* to *-i*. Then add the ending for the tense.

EXAMPLES	I **worry** sometimes.
	She never **worries**.
	He **worried** all day.

Activity G Write the correct tense of the verb in the parentheses to complete each sentence.

1) Yesterday Kim (play) tennis.

2) Andy (apply) for a job last week.

3) Melissa (buy) a new outfit once a month.

4) Last year James (work) on the school newspaper.

5) Eric (enjoy) last week's football game.

6) This morning they (hurry) to school.

7) Sandra (reply) to Aunt Emily's letter.

8) Yesterday he (stay) home from school.

9) That loud thunder (terrify) me.

10) The witness (testify) for two days during the trial.

The past participle is the third part of the verb. It is used with *have, has,* or *had* to form the perfect tenses of irregular verbs. Look at these commonly used irregular verbs.

EXAMPLES	Present	Past	Past Participle
	begin	began	(have) begun
	catch	caught	(have) caught
	choose	chose	(have) chosen
	come	came	(have) come
	eat	ate	(have) eaten
	give	gave	(have) given
	go	went	(have) gone
	know	knew	(have) known
	see	saw	(have) seen
	teach	taught	(have) taught

Activity H   Write the past or past participle form of the verb in parentheses to complete each sentence.

1) Ms. Lee has (teach) math for many years.

2) Carol (give) her old bike to her sister.

3) Leon (see) an old friend at the movies.

4) They have already (eat) their dinner.

5) Have you ever (see) that movie?

6) Phillip had (begin) his homework already.

7) Jackie (know) the answer to the question.

8) The fielder (catch) the deep fly ball.

9) The news (come) on TV at six o'clock.

10) Where has Monica (go)?

11) Saturday everyone (go) to the game.

12) I have (choose) a partner for the assignment.

The words in a verb phrase are usually written together. However, they may be separated by another word or words in the sentence.

She **has** finally **written** the letter.

Has Donna really **gone** to the library?

Michael **will** probably **finish** his homework after the game.

Activity I   Write the verb phrase in each of these sentences on your paper. Ignore any words that come between the helping verb and the main verb.

1) James has always given his best.

2) Have you ever heard that song before?

3) Victor has often seen him at the field.

4) I had not met her before today.

5) Have you ever studied Spanish?

6) Carl will probably bring his lunch.

7) Jane and Sam have never gone to an art museum.

8) Connie had seldom enjoyed a book so much.

Activity J   Write the tense of each bold verb or verb phrase on your paper.

1) **Will** you **drive** me to the store?

2) Yesterday Beth **lost** her gloves.

3) Ms. Potter **teaches** my math class.

4) The coach finally **chose** all of the players.

5) Melissa **had known** most of the players for years.

6) A reporter **has written** about many of our games.

7) His latest story **will appear** in tomorrow's paper.

8) By noon everyone in town **will have read** it.

Lesson Review Write the all the verbs and verb phrases in the story below on your paper. Beside each verb or verb phrase, write its tense.

Wildcats devour Lincoln Lions

On Saturday, September 30, the Wilson Wildcat fans enjoyed a 21-3 victory over the Lincoln Lions.

Quarterback George Benetez threw two touchdown passes in the first half. The half ended at 14-0. The Lions' only score came in the third quarter with a field goal.

James Melcher made a big play late in the final quarter. He tackled the Lions' running back. The running back fumbled the ball. The Wildcats recovered on their 48-yard line. Wilson marched down the field and scored the final goal. Many fans will have already extended congratulations to Melcher. We offer ours now for a fine play.

Next week the Wildcats will face the Crofton Cougers. The team hopes for a winning season. They have looked forward to the county championship for many years.

The Progressive Forms

Progressive form

The form of a verb that ends in -ing *and uses a form of the verb* be *as a helping verb to show continuing action.*

The **progressive forms** of verbs express continuing action. Compare the two sentences below.

Present   Melissa **practices** the trumpet twice a week.

                                 (Shows an action that is done frequently.)

Present progressive   Melissa **is practicing** the trumpet.

                                 (Shows an action that is being done now.)

The fourth part of the verb has the ending *-ing* and is called the present participle.

EXAMPLES	Present	Present Participle
	work	working
	see	seeing
	be	being

A progressive form is a verb phrase. It is made from a form of the verb *be* plus the present participle.

EXAMPLES

Present progressive:	He **is working**.
Past progressive:	He **was working**.
Future progressive:	He **will be working**.
Present perfect progressive:	He **has been working**.
Past perfect progressive:	He **had been working**.
Future perfect progressive:	He **will have been working**.

Activity A   Write the verb phrase in each of these sentences on your paper.

1) Hai Sin was practicing her flute when the phone rang.
2) Soon Tom will be practicing the drums.
3) Sam has been practicing for thirty minutes.
4) Cathy had been practicing the trumpet when I interrupted her.
5) In five minutes, the band will have been practicing for an hour.

Verbs form their progressive form by adding -*ing* to the present tense and using the helping verb *be*.

Be is an irregular verb.

You need to know the different forms of *be* to form the progressive tense of verbs.

(To) Be

Simple Tenses

Present	**Past**	**Future**
I am	I was	I shall be
you are	you were	you will be
he is	he was	he will be
we are	we were	we shall be
you are	you were	you will be
they are	they were	they will be

Perfect Tenses

Present Perfect	**Past Perfect**	**Future Perfect**
I have been	I had been	I shall have been
you have been	you had been	you will have been
he has been	he had been	he will have been
we have been	we had been	we shall have been
you have been	you had been	you will have been
they have been	they had been	they will have been

Activity B   Write on your paper the correct form of the verb *be* to complete each sentence.

1) I have _____ on an airplane six times.

2) Jack will _____ going to Seattle next week.

3) Doris has _____ in my class every year.

4) By noon, Mac will have _____ working for four hours.

5) Sara _____ leaving for Florida on Friday.

Activity C   Write a sentence for each of these verbs on your paper.

1) will have been going

2) has been working

3) had been eating

4) is beginning

5) were whispering

6) am opening

Activity D   Write the tense of each bold verb phrase on your paper.

1) Mario **had** never **gone** to Texas before this year.

2) He **is flying** there for a vacation.

3) He **will be leaving** at noon.

4) Mario **has been packing** all morning.

5) They **are going** to the airport now.

Activity E   Write a sentence for each verb, using the tense given in parentheses. Underline the verb or verb phrase in your sentence.

Example   pass (present progressive)
            Ted is passing the salad to Bill.

1) drive   (future progressive)

2) have   (past progressive)

3) fish   (present progressive)

4) see   (future perfect progressive)

5) pour   (past perfect progressive)

6) go   (simple past)

7) wonder   (present perfect progressive)

8) jump   (present perfect)

Activity F Write the verb that should appear in each sentence to make it correct.

Examples Use the present participle (verb + *-ing*) with any forms of the helping verb *be*.
Sheila **is fixing** her bike.

Use the past participle form (verb + *-ed*) with any forms of the helping verb *have*.
Sheila **has fixed** her bike.

If the verb phrase includes both *have* and *be*, use the present participle (verb + *-ing*).
Sheila **has been fixing** her bike.

1) Rosa has been (playing, played) the trumpet for several years.

2) She has (playing, played) in the Wilson band for two years.

3) This year the band is (going, gone) to Florida for a national contest.

4) Some of the parents will be (accompanying, accompanied) the band.

5) The band members have been (raising, raised) money all year.

6) So far they have (raising, raised) more than one thousand dollars.

7) Everyone is (selling, sold) school t-shirts.

8) So far, they have (selling, sold) a thousand items.

9) Rosa herself has (buying, bought) t-shirts for her mom and her two sisters.

10) She will be (giving, gave) them as birthday presents.

Lesson 3 Review

Part A Write sentences on your paper using the verb *sharpen* in each of the six regular tenses and the six progressive forms. *Sharpen* is a regular verb. The first one has been done for you.

1) present—Phillip **sharpens** his pencil before class.
2) past
3) future
4) present perfect
5) past perfect
6) future perfect
7) present progressive
8) past progressive
9) future progressive
10) present perfect progressive
11) past perfect progressive
12) future perfect progressive

Part B Write the verbs or verb phrases in this paragraph on your paper. Beside each verb or verb phrase, write its tense.

Louis Armstrong played the trumpet. He earned a special place in American history. As a child, he lived in an orphanage in New Orleans. There he first studied the cornet. In 1922, he played on a Mississippi riverboat. He joined a band in Chicago. Then in 1924, Armstrong moved to New York City. Soon he was playing the trumpet. He invented a completely new style. By 1925, he was recording his music. Later he formed his own band. People also loved his husky voice. In the 1930s, Armstrong starred in movies. His popularity continued for the rest of his life. One of his records, "Hello, Dolly!" sold two million copies in 1964. Armstrong died in 1971. People will remember this man and his music for a long time.

The helping verbs *do* and *did* are used with a negative word, such as *not*.

 Many stores **do** *not* **close** on holidays. (present)

Dan **did** *not* **find** his book. (past)

The helping verbs *do* and *did* also are used to form questions.

 Do you **like** strawberries? (present)

Did you **finish** that book? (past)

The helping verbs *do* and *did* are used only with the present form of the main verb.

 Did you **go** home? (The verb *go* is present.)

The verb *do* can also be used as a main verb. The main verb *do* means "to perform an action." It can be used in all tenses.

EXAMPLES	Present:	Brigette **does** her chores early.
	Past:	Victor **did** his work well.
	Future:	Everyone **will do** his part.
	Present perfect:	The family **has done** its work well.
	Past perfect:	We **had done** the yard work by dinnertime.
	Future perfect:	Soon he **will have done** his lessons.

Activity A Write all the verbs and their helpers in these sentences on your paper.

1) Did you see Anita at lunch?

2) Jack never did find his gloves.

3) The family is doing the dishes.

4) Do you read the newspaper?

5) Where do you do your homework?

Activity B Write the bold verb in these sentences on your paper. Beside it, write whether *do* is a helping verb, a main verb, or both.

Example   Soon he **will have done** his report.

                will have done—main verb

1) After dinner Eric and Melissa **did** the dishes.

2) Finally they **had done** all their chores.

3) Melissa **had** already **done** her homework.

4) "**Did** you **see** my math book?" Eric asked.

5) "What **did** you **do** with it this time?" she asked.

6) "I **did** not **see** it today," he said.

7) **Did** Eric ever **find** his book?

8) Soon he **was doing** his math.

Part A Write the verb or verb phrase in each of these sentences on your paper.

1) Yesterday, Tanya did her yard work.

2) She was doing yard work all afternoon.

3) Soon she will have done the entire yard.

4) She had done all of the weeding, too.

5) Did Tanya complete her tasks?

6) Who does the yard work at your house?

Part B Write the verb or verb phrase in each of these sentences on your paper. Beside each verb or verb phrase, write its tense.

1) In the fall, people do extra yard work.

2) Did you rake your leaves yet?

3) They have already raked their yard.

4) Does your family plant grass seed in the fall?

5) Soon they will have done the whole yard.

6) I have already done my part.

7) Did Dad do the front yard?

8) The boys are doing the pruning.

9) They did not trim the fruit trees this year.

10) How does the yard look?

The Conditional Forms

Some helping verbs put a condition on an action. A condition is a requirement or a responsibility.

EXAMPLES	May—Might	He **may** succeed.
		He **might** succeed.
	Can—Could	He **can** sing.
		He **could** sing.
	Shall—Should	You **shall** leave.
		You **should** leave.
	Will—Would	The basket **will** hold a bushel.
		He **would** like that movie.
	Must	I **must** go now.
		You **must** find your paper.
		They **must** leave quickly.

Now, look carefully at the main verbs in the verb phrases above. They are all present tense verbs.

Activity A   Write the verb phrase in each of these sentences on your paper.

1) You may stay at the party until ten o'clock.

2) Mo can play the trombone.

3) The basket will hold a dozen tomatoes.

4) She should do her homework.

5) She must finish her report tonight.

6) I would like that play.

7) They could join us for dinner.

8) We might try that new food.

The **conditional forms** of helping verbs are irregular. Do NOT add an -s to the verb when you use it with a singular subject.

EXAMPLES

Singular Subject	Plural Subject
He **may** go.	They **may** go.
Jack **must** leave.	The men **must** leave.

All of the other regular verbs and irregular verbs DO either add an -s or change to a different form.

EXAMPLES

Singular Subject	Plural Subject
He **sings** well.	They **sing** well.
He **has gone**.	They **have gone**.
She **is going**.	They **are going**.

The conditional form may be combined with the compound tenses.

EXAMPLES

Present perfect tense:	I **have gone**.
Conditional form:	I **could have gone**.
	He **might have gone**.
Present progressive form:	I **am going**.
Conditional progressive form:	I **could be going**.
	They **must be going**.

In some sentences, the main verb is not stated. It is understood.

EXAMPLES

Are you doing your homework?

No, but I should. (The rest of the verb phrase, *do my homework,* is understood.)

Activity B Write the verb that should appear in each sentence to make it correct.

1) Every day Andy (exercise, exercises) at the gym.

2) They (exercise, exercises) on a regular basis.

3) Julian (might, mights) exercise today.

4) He would (goes, go) every day if he had the time.

Activity C Write the verb phrase in each of these sentences on your paper.

1) Cam's purse will hold many things.

2) She should clean it up.

3) In fact, she must clean it up.

4) She cannot find anything in it.

5) Cam should have bought a new purse.

6) She might be buying a new one.

7) Should she buy a new purse?

8) Yes, she should.

Part A   Write the verb or verb phrase in each of these sentences on your paper.

1) Next week, I might be going to Indiana.

2) I could have gone last year.

3) This year I must go.

4) I would leave on Monday if possible.

5) I should pack my bags.

6) I must take my winter coat.

7) I can go by plane.

8) I may take only one bag.

9) Should I take an umbrella?

10) It might rain.

Part B   Write a conditional helping verb on your paper to complete each sentence.

1) Suke _____ go to the movies with Danny.

2) Danny _____ ask her to go.

3) Al _____ finish his work by noon.

4) He _____ finish sooner if he hurries.

5) Lily said that Erin _____ use the school computer.

6) With a computer, Erin _____ write a better paper.

7) That computer program _____ catch grammar and spelling errors.

8) Gerry _____ like that program.

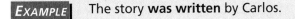

Active verb

A verb that is used if the subject does the action.

Use an **active verb** if the subject is doing the action. The sentence tells who did what.

> EXAMPLE   Carlos **wrote** a story.

Passive verb

A verb that is used when the action happens to the subject.

Use a **passive verb** if the action happens to the subject. The sentence tells what was done by whom.

> EXAMPLE   The story **was written** by Carlos.

To form the passive verb, use the helping verb *be* with the past participle (the third part of the verb).

> EXAMPLE   Correct: The story **was written** by Carlos.
>
> Incorrect: The story **was wrote** by Carlos.

In some sentences that use passive voice, the person doing the action is not named. The person is "understood."

> EXAMPLES   Today the bank **was robbed**.   (by someone)
>
> The pass **was thrown** well.   (by someone)

Activity A   Write the verbs and their helpers in these sentences on your paper.

1) The note was discovered by Mary.

2) We were disturbed by a loud noise.

3) The telephone was finally answered.

4) The ball was hit to left field.

5) The car was greased last month.

Activity B   Write the verbs in these sentences on your paper. Beside each verb, write whether it is *active* or *passive*.

1) John Steinbeck wrote many stories.

2) *The Red Pony* was written by John Steinbeck.

3) Edgar Allan Poe wrote many poems.

4) "The Raven" was written by Poe.

5) That cake was baked by my aunt.

6) My aunt baked that cake.

Activity C   Write two sentences for each of these verbs on your paper. In the first sentence, use the word as an active verb. In the second sentence, use the word as a passive verb.

1) cover	**6)** hit
2) direct	**7)** invent
3) discover	**8)** cook
4) disturb	**9)** answer
5) teach	**10)** pack

Part A Write the verb and any helper in these sentences on your paper.

1) The cotton gin was invented by Eli Whitney.

2) Cotton seeds are removed from the cotton.

3) In 1842, the Oregon Trail was explored by John Fremont.

4) Fremont was later elected as one of California's first senators.

5) *Gone With the Wind* was written by Margaret Mitchell.

6) Her book was made into a successful movie.

7) Indiana was settled in 1808 by Tecumseh, a Shawnee leader.

8) Tecumseh was killed at the battle of the Thames in Canada during the War of 1812.

9) In 1848, Lewis Cass was defeated by Zachary Taylor.

10) Taylor was elected as President of the United States.

Part B Rewrite each of these sentences on your paper. Change the verb in bold from passive to active.

Example Passive: The cotton gin **was invented** by Eli Whitney.

Active: Eli Whitney **invented** the cotton gin.

1) The batter **was hit** by the wild pitch.

2) John's bag **was packed** by his mother.

3) The telephone **was answered** by the receptionist.

4) The neighbors **were disturbed** by the barking dog.

5) The oil **was changed** last month by the mechanic.

Part A   Write the verb or verb phrase in each of these sentences on your paper.

1) George Herman Ruth began his baseball career in 1914.

2) His teammates gave him the nickname "Babe."

3) He first played with the minor league Baltimore Orioles.

4) Baltimore sold his contract to the Boston Red Sox.

5) Babe pitched and batted left-handed.

6) In 1919, he broke all of the records for home runs in a season.

7) The New York Yankees had been looking at Ruth for some time.

8) In 1920, he was sent to the Yankees.

9) He would play in games in the outfield.

10) He led the league in home runs for many years.

11) He was hitting more home runs every year.

12) In 1927, he set a new world record.

13) He had hit sixty home runs in a single year.

14) In his last game, Babe Ruth hit three home runs in a row.

15) He was elected to the Baseball Hall of Fame in 1936.

Part B   Number your paper from 1 to 25. Write the verb that should appear in each sentence to make it correct.

1) Mr. Torres (went, gone) to work.

2) The Wildcats will (play, played) their first game on Saturday.

3) The team (practice, practices) every day.

4) They (want, wants) a victory.

5) Everyone (like, likes) to win.

6) He (have, has) never had an injury.

7) They have (score, scored) two touchdowns.

8) Monday they (hurryed, hurried) to work.

9) Last week the man (testifies, testified) at the trial.

10) I have (beginned, begun) my work.

11) He (bring, brings) his lunch every day.

12) Yvonne (knowed, knew) the answer.

13) Sara always (do, does) her work well.

14) The band (is, are) practicing now.

15) The children (is, are) riding their bikes.

16) He (be, is) flying to Florida.

17) Did you (finish, finished) that book?

18) Did Juan (go, went) home yet?

19) He (must, musts) go home now.

20) Janine (is, could) be finished by noon.

21) The book was (wrote, written) by Jack London.

22) That cake was (bake, baked) by Bob.

23) The electric lightbulb was (inventing, invented) by Thomas Edison.

24) We (was, were) disturbed by the bell.

25) The barking dog (make, made) everyone angry.

Test Taking Tip Before you answer any question on an exam, skim through the whole test to find out what is expected of you.

The State-of-Being Verb

When you discuss relationships and feelings, you may say sentences such as these: I *am* their son. The food *tastes* wonderful.

A verb is a word that expresses action or a state of being. A state-of-being verb tells something about the condition or state of the subject of the sentence.

In Chapter 5, you will learn about state-of-being verbs. Each lesson in the chapter focuses on the correct use and form of state-of-being verbs in sentences.

Goals for Learning

▶ To identify state-of-being verbs and verb phrases in sentences

▶ To distinguish between active and state-of-being verbs and verb phrases in sentences

▶ To identify the correct form of state-of-being verbs in sentences

State-of-being verb

A verb that explains or describes the subject of a sentence. A state-of-being verb is also called a linking verb.

A **state-of-being verb** tells something about the condition or state of the subject of the sentence. A state-of-being verb does not tell what the subject is doing. State-of-being verbs are also called linking verbs.

EXAMPLES

State-of-being verb: Roberto **is** a tackle on the football team.

Action verb: Roberto **plays** on the football team.

In the first sentence, the verb *is* helps to make a statement about Roberto. In the second sentence, the verb *plays* tells the action that Roberto does.

The most common state-of-being verb is *be* and all its forms: *am, is, are, was, were, be, being, been. To be* means "to exist, to live, or to happen."

Here are some other commonly used state-of-being, or linking, verbs:

appear	grow	seem
become	keep	smell
feel	look	stay
get	remain	taste

Activity A   Read the examples. Then write five more sentences about Roberto on your paper. Use state-of-being verbs. Underline the verb in each sentence.

Examples   Roberto **seems** nice.
Roberto **is** a student.
Roberto **grew** tall.
Roberto **gets** taller every year.
Roberto **looks** friendly.

The verb *be* can also be a helping verb. It can be used with a main verb to express progressive tenses.

EXAMPLES	Jamie **is cooking** dinner.
	Eric **was talking** softly.

In addition, *be* is used to form passive verbs. *Be* is a helping verb in those verb phrases, too.

EXAMPLE	The picture **was painted** by Norman Rockwell.

Activity B   Write the verb or verb phrase in each of these sentences on your paper. Beside each verb or verb phrase, write whether the verb *be* is a main verb or a helping verb.

1) Dawn was feeling fine yesterday.
2) Today she is sick.
3) She is going to the doctor.
4) Dawn will be absent from school.
5) She will probably be better tomorrow.

Be is almost always a state-of-being verb when it is the main verb of the sentence. Some other state-of-being verbs can also express an action. If you can substitute a form of *be* for these verbs, they are state-of-being verbs. If not, they are action verbs.

EXAMPLES	State-of-being verb:	The stew **tasted** good. (You could say: The stew *was* good.)
	Action verb:	Michael **tasted** the stew. (You cannot say: Michael *was* the stew.)

Activity C   Write the verb or verb phrase in each of these sentences on your paper. Beside each verb or verb phrase, write whether it is an *action verb* or a *state-of-being verb*.

1) The old house smelled musty and stale.
2) The children were smelling the flowers.
3) The boys grew beans, squash, and corn in their garden.
4) Your body will grow stronger with exercise.
5) He feels sick.

State-of-being verbs also express tense.

EXAMPLES		
	Present:	The water **feels** warm.
	Past:	He **looked** good yesterday.
	Future:	Mary **will be** fifteen next week.
	Present perfect:	I **have been** hungry all day.
	Past perfect:	Jack **had seemed** tired by dinnertime.
	Future perfect:	Carol **will have been** sick for a week tomorrow.

Activity D   Write the verb or verb phrase in each of these sentences on your paper. Beside each verb or verb phrase, write its tense.

1) "The Tell-Tale Heart" is an interesting story.

2) Sam will not be happy about that.

3) Mrs. Franco has been our neighbor for two years.

4) She was a Spanish teacher.

5) We had been the winners twice.

6) We will have become tired by then.

7) The cloth had felt smooth and soft.

8) They have been asleep all morning.

9) This plant grows best in the shade.

10) Did Mr. Lee seem upset to you?

State-of-being verbs may be used in the progressive form. Use the verb *be* as a helping verb. Then use the present participle form (*-ing*) of the verb.

> **EXAMPLES**　It **is staying** warm today.
>
> 　　　　　　I **will be feeling** fine soon.

Activity E　Write the present participle for each state-of-being verb below on your paper. Then write a sentence for each verb.

Example　grow—growing　I **am growing** taller this year.

1) be

2) seem

3) appear

4) look

5) feel

6) become

Conditional helping verbs may be used with state-of-being verbs.

> **EXAMPLES**　Karl **must be** in love.
>
> 　　　　　　The dog **could become** angry.

Activity F　Write the state-of-being verb or verb phrase in each of these sentences on your paper.

1) Ron and Jamie were ready for Thanksgiving.

2) The roast turkey would taste good.

3) The pumpkin pies in the oven smelled delicious.

4) Everything looked wonderful.

5) "Is dinner ready yet?"

6) The whole family was hungry.

7) "I have been very hungry all day!"

8) Dinner was great!

9) The conversation around the table sounded happy.

Part A   Write the verb or verb phrase in each of these sentences on your paper.

1) My aunt is eighty years old.

2) She is looking well.

3) She always has felt healthy.

4) Aunt Marie is a good cook.

5) She has been keeping very active.

Part B   Write the verb or verb phrase in each of these sentences on your paper. Beside each verb or verb phrase, write whether it is an *action verb* or a *state-of-being verb*.

Example   Debbie tasted the turkey.   **tasted—action**

Dinner will be ready soon.   **will be—state-of-being**

1) Dinner was served at three o'clock.

2) The food looked wonderful.

3) That turkey smells delicious.

4) The drumstick is my favorite part.

5) The sweet potatoes tasted quite fine.

6) May I have more corn?

7) My grandmother looks pleased.

8) I feel full.

9) My parents seem extra quiet.

10) They must be tired from all the cooking.

The verb *be* is almost always a state-of-being verb when it is the main verb in a sentence.

EXAMPLES

The turkey **is** golden brown.

The turkey **is** delicious.

Many other state-of-being verbs can be used as action verbs.

EXAMPLES

Jamie **tasted** the cranberry sauce.
(action verb)

The cranberry sauce **tasted** sweet.
(state-of-being verb)

In the first sentence, *tasted* expresses action. Jamie did something. In the second sentence, *tasted* expresses a state of being. The condition of the cranberry sauce was sweet.

Here are examples of the different uses of several state-of-being verbs.

EXAMPLES

APPEAR

action: to come into view; to become visible

Jack **appeared** suddenly.
The actor **appeared** on the stage.

being: to seem; to look

They **appear** friendly.
Fred **appears** taller than Mike.

FEEL

action: to touch; to think or believe

She **felt** the soft blanket.
I **feel** that you are right.

being: to be aware of a physical or mental sensation

I **feel** cold.
Denny **feels** happy.

GROW

action: to cause to grow; to cultivate

I **grew** tomatoes in my garden.
The farmer **grows** corn.

being: to come into existence; to spring up

Don **grew** two inches this year.
The day **grew** cold.

SMELL

action: to catch the scent or odor of something

I could **smell** the fresh mountain air.
I **smell** popcorn.

being: to have a certain scent or odor

The bread **smells** delicious.
The skunk **smells** awful.

Activity A   Write whether the verb in bold in each of these sentences expresses *action* or a *state of being*.

1) She could **smell** the smoke in the air.

2) The warm cake **smelled** inviting.

3) The oven **felt** too hot.

4) Mary **felt** a hole in her pocket.

5) Joe **grows** orange trees in Arizona.

6) She **appeared** to have a good time.

7) She **has grown** as tall as I.

8) Our cat **smells** his food before he tastes it.

9) Brad **felt** wonderful about his perfect score.

10) Nora suddenly **appeared** at the party.

If you are not sure whether a verb is a state-of-being verb, remember to try this test. Substitute a form of the verb *be* or *seem* for the verb. If the meaning of the sentence is almost the same, the verb is a state-of-being verb. You cannot substitute a form of *be* for an action verb.

EXAMPLES	State-of-being verb:	They **remained** friends.
		They **were** friends.
	Action verb:	He **got** a new job.
		He **was** a new job.
		(not possible)

Activity B Write two sentences for each of these verbs on your paper. In the first sentence, use the verb as an action verb. In the second sentence, use the verb as a state-of-being verb.

appear	feel	grow	look
taste	get	keep	smell

Activity C   Remember that a state-of-being verb does not tell what the subject is doing. It does not express action. Write on your paper whether each verb in bold in these sentences expresses *action* or a *state of being*.

1) Their whole family **is** healthy.

2) Mrs. Jones **is reading** a book.

3) Ron **is** asleep on the sofa.

4) He **seems** tired this evening!

5) Mr. Jones **stays** awake.

6) He **is eating** an apple.

7) He **likes** a snack in the evening.

8) Jamie **appears** very busy.

9) She **must be doing** homework.

10) The television **is** loud.

Activity D   Write the verb or verb phrase in each of these sentences on your paper. Beside each verb or verb phrase, write whether it expresses *action* or a *state of being*.

Examples   She tasted the soup.   **tasted—action**

               Dinner will be ready soon.   **will be—state of being**

1) Smell these beautiful flowers.

2) The grass seems greener this time of year.

3) Food always tastes better at the beach.

4) That cute little puppy in the window is watching us.

5) This has been a very dry summer.

6) The plants in our garden became yellow and shriveled.

7) I am saving for a new CD player.

8) At this time tomorrow, we will be hiking up a mountain.

9) Did you taste the vegetable pizza?

10) How were you feeling yesterday?

Part A   Write whether the bold verb in these sentences expresses *action* or a *state of being*.

1) Howard finally **appeared**.

2) He **appears** strong and healthy.

3) I **felt** the soft cloth.

4) The cloth **felt** soft to me.

5) She **looked** everywhere for her cat.

6) Her cat **looked** frightened.

7) The oak tree **grew** eight feet tall.

8) I **grow** radishes in my garden every year.

Part B   Write the verb or verb phrase in each of these sentences on your paper. Beside each verb or verb phrase, write whether it expresses *action* or a *state of being*.

1) Mr. Klein was looking for the newspaper.

2) He usually keeps it on the coffee table.

3) That paper gets harder to find every day.

4) Suddenly the newspaper appeared!

5) The newspaper appeared wrinkled.

6) It also looked torn.

7) "Who got this paper before me?"

8) Mr. Klein grew thoughtful for a moment.

9) He spotted the dog under the table.

10) "Some dogs are frisky."

11) Then he smiled.

12) The newspaper was not damaged that much.

13) He remained in his chair with his newspaper for a while.

14) He got the news of the day.

A state-of-being verb must agree with its subject. Regular verbs and most irregular verbs add an -*s* or -*es* to the present form when the subject is singular.

EXAMPLE	Singular Subject	Plural Subject
	Jack **looks** happy.	They **look** happy.

The past form of the verb stays the same for singular and plural subjects.

EXAMPLE	Singular Subject	Plural Subject
	Donna **looked** nice.	Both girls **looked** nice.

The verb *be* is an irregular verb.

Singular	**Present**	**Past**
First person	I **am**	I **was**
Second person	you **are**	you **were**
Third person	he **is**	he **was**
Plural		
First person	we **are**	we **were**
Second person	you **are**	you **were**
Third person	they **are**	they **were**

Activity A   Each of these sentences contains a form of the verb *be*. Write the verb and its form on your paper.

Example   He is Michelle's brother.
is—third person, singular, present

1) I am busy today.
2) They were happy to get the award.
3) They are friends of mine.
4) She is a careful driver.
5) The crowd was anxious for the game to be over.
6) We were excited about our trip.

The past participle of *be* is *been*. Use *been* with *have, has,* and *had* to form the perfect tenses.

> **EXAMPLES**
>
> Fred **has been** sick.
>
> They **have been** busy all day.
>
> Mike **had been** their helper.

The present participle of *be* is *being*. Use *being* with the helping verb *be* to show the progressive form.

> **EXAMPLES**
>
> Donna **is being** nice.
>
> Jack **was being** friendly.

Activity B   Write the correct form of the verb *be* in each sentence on your paper.

1) Megan's report _____ due yesterday.
2) They _____ unhappy about my decision.
3) Has he ever _____ a teacher?
4) Yellowstone Park in Wyoming _____ a national park.
5) The children were _____ silly.
6) "You _____ our next patient," the nurse said.
7) I had never _____ a guest in their house before.

Use the verb *be* to show future tense and to show simple conditional forms.

> **EXAMPLES**
>
> Future: He **will be** home soon.
>
> Conditional: Jamie **must be** late.

Activity C   Write the correct form of the verb *be* in each sentence on your paper.

1) Will you _____ my project partner?
2) I should _____ more careful.
3) Must I always _____ the first one?
4) Can I _____ the last one?
5) Howard will _____ disappointed about the game.

Here are some common mistakes to avoid:

1. Sometimes people leave out the *be* verb or part of the verb phrase in a sentence.

EXAMPLES	Incorrect:	The quarterback fast!
	Correct:	The quarterback **is** fast!
	Incorrect:	I be ready soon.
	Correct:	I **will be** ready soon.

2. Sometimes people use *be* instead of the correct present form.

EXAMPLES	Incorrect:	They be good friends.
	Correct:	They **are** good friends.
	Incorrect:	Roberto be my brother.
	Correct:	Roberto **is** my brother.

Activity D   Each of these sentences contains a mistake with the use of the verb *be*. Write each sentence correctly on your paper.

1) "Where Roberto?" Stacy asked.

2) "They be practicing late today," she said.

3) "He be a good quarterback," Sam said.

4) "We be going to the mall after school."

5) "Roberto be tired after practice," Sam told her.

Lesson Review   Write the correct form of the verb *be* in each of these sentences on your paper.

1) In November there _____ a contest at Wilson High School.

2) Jun _____ entering the contest.

3) She wanted to _____ the winner of the band scholarship.

4) Her talent _____ playing the tuba.

5) Sixty other students _____ part of the contest.

6) On the night of the contest, Jun's parents _____ excited.

7) Before the contest, Jun had _____ nervous.

8) When she came on stage to play her tuba, she _____ calm.

9) Later, she _____ asked about her future plans.

10) She had _____ thinking about this a lot.

11) "Who will _____ the winner?"

12) Finally, the winners _____ announced.

13) "Jun Tan has _____ chosen as the winner of the Wilson High Band scholarship."

14) Mr. and Mrs. Tan _____ very proud.

15) So _____ her brother Adam.

16) Jun must _____ the happiest of all!

Part A   Write the verb or verb phrase in each of these sentences on your paper.

1) The last days of November grew cold.

2) Winter winds felt chilly.

3) The days were growing shorter.

4) The sky became dark early in the evening.

5) The cool air smelled fresh and clean.

6) On most days the sky was clear.

7) There was little rain that autumn.

8) Soon the first snowfall would come.

9) Everyone was feeling full of energy.

10) It was a pleasant time of the year.

Part B   Write the verb or verb phrase in each of these sentences on your paper. Beside each verb or verb phrase, write whether it expresses *action* or a *state of being*.

1) The weather in December stayed cold.

2) People got out their winter coats.

3) "It gets cold earlier every year," Dave complained.

4) One day the sky looked gray.

5) "I can smell snow in the air," said Eli.

6) "It feels too cold for it to snow," Dave said.

7) "Hey! I felt a snowflake," said Eli.

8) They looked in Dave's garage for his sled.

9) The sky grew darker.

10) The snow was getting heavier.

Part C Write the correct form of the verb *be* in each of these sentences on your paper.

1) "It definitely _____ snowing," Eli said.

2) "I _____ ready to go sledding," Dave said.

3) Soon the snow _____ deep enough.

4) They had _____ sledding for an hour.

5) They should _____ going home for dinner.

Part D Write the word that should appear in each sentence to make it correct.

1) Will Carol (be, been) at the meeting tomorrow?

2) She (be, is) almost always on time.

3) They (is, are) old friends of Jason's.

4) The puppy is (been, being) quiet today.

5) I (was, were) thinking about tomorrow's math test.

6) Everyone (was, were) happy about the news.

7) You have always (be, been) my best friend.

8) Al (seem, seems) glad about the new car.

9) Both of the pies (smell, smells) very good.

10) (Is, Are) your last name Miller?

Test Taking Tip Spend time studying new material for several days or weeks before a test. Don't try to learn new material the night before a test.

Chapter

6

The Adverb

When you are describing people, places, and events, you often use adjectives. You may also want to add descriptive details about *how, when,* or *how often* the event happened. Then you need to use different kinds of describing words.

An adverb is a word that answers questions about a verb, an adjective, or another adverb.

In Chapter 6, you will learn about adverbs. Each lesson in the chapter focuses on recognizing and using adverbs correctly in sentences.

Goals for Learning

▶ To identify adverbs in sentences
▶ To identify the word that the adverb answers questions about
▶ To use adverbs correctly to make comparisons

Adverb

A word that answers questions about a verb, an adjective, or another adverb. It tells How? When? Where? How often? How long? *or* How many times?

An **adverb** is a word that answers questions about a verb, an adjective, or another adverb. An adverb tells *how, when, where,* or *how much.*

Adverbs that answer the question *How?* are usually used with action verbs. They tell something about the way the action was done.

EXAMPLES

The dog barked **loudly**.

They did the assignment **correctly**.

Jack guessed **right**.

Carla works **quickly**.

Activity A Write these sentences on your paper. Add an adverb that answers the question *How was the action done?* about the verb in bold.

1) The family **ate** their dinner _____ .

2) Willis **drives** his car _____ .

3) May **sews** _____ .

4) Mrs. Barrett **sang** _____ .

5) We **cleaned** the house _____ .

Activity B Write on your paper the adverb that answers the question *How?* in each of these sentences.

1) The ballerina danced gracefully.

2) The acrobat climbed the ladder quickly.

3) Gail helped us gladly.

4) Slowly Ella found the answers.

5) Juan played the game hard.

6) Anna plays the piano well.

7) I got home fast.

8) She sewed the hem straight.

Adverbs also answer these questions: *When? How often? How long?* or *How many times?*

They tell something about the time of the action or state of being.

I am leaving town **today**.

Sarah will be home **soon**.

I would like to go to the beach **again**.

John will speak **next**.

Carol is **usually** happy.

Adverbs also answer the questions *Where?* or *In what direction?* They tell something about the place of the action or state of being.

Lloyd lives **here**.

Leave your coat **downstairs**.

You should turn **left**.

Activity C   Write each adverb below in a sentence on your paper. Underline the adverb in each sentence.

1) often

2) tomorrow

3) never

4) still

5) yesterday

6) today

7) now

8) always

9) later

10) twice

11) already

12) again

Activity D Write the adverbs in each of these sentences on your paper. The adverbs answer the questions *When?* or *How often?*

1) Please begin immediately!

2) I will go first.

3) They jumped up instantly.

4) Our parents seldom go to the movies.

5) I saw the movie before.

6) The weather has been nice lately.

7) Sometimes I enjoy golf.

8) Occasionally we visit our relatives in Texas.

9) The newspaper is delivered daily.

10) We trim our trees yearly.

Activity E Write the adverbs in each of these sentences on your paper. The adverbs answer the questions *Where?* or *In what direction?*

1) The team advanced the ball forward.

2) Please go away.

3) Turn right at the corner.

4) Hang your coats here.

5) The bedrooms are upstairs.

6) They looked at the stars above.

7) The storm was near.

Part A Write all the adverbs in these sentences on your paper. A sentence may have more than one adverb.

1) Yesterday, the dog happily buried his bone.

2) Today, he looked for it.

3) He barked loudly for Carla.

4) "I bet you lost your bone again," Carla scolded gently.

5) The dog jumped up and down constantly.

6) Jokingly she said, "Sometimes you are a silly dog."

7) Finally, Carla found the bone.

8) She gave it to the dog quickly.

9) Immediately, he ran away with it.

10) "Be careful with it now!" she reminded him.

Part B Complete each sentence by writing an adverb that answers the question in parentheses about the verb in bold.

1) The students **rushed** to their desks (How?).

2) (How often?), their teacher **gave** them a surprise quiz.

3) Otis **came** in late (How often?).

4) Mr. Wang **walked** (Where?).

5) The silence seemed to **last** (How long?).

Adverbs that answer questions about adjectives and other adverbs are called adverbs of degree. They answer these questions: *How much? How little? How often?* and *To what degree?*

EXAMPLES	It is **very** cold here.

It is **very** cold here.

The adverb *very* tells about the adjective *cold*.

How cold is it?

It is **very** cold!

I work **extremely** fast.

The adverb *extremely* tells about the adverb *fast*.

How fast?

Extremely fast!

The adverb of degree is usually placed before the adjective or adverb.

Activity A   Write these sentences on your paper. Circle the adverbs of degree.

1) His old truck is so noisy.

2) Your puppy is quite friendly.

3) That is an unusually large pumpkin.

4) What a very funny movie that was!

5) He has an extremely bad headache.

6) I am especially tired this morning.

7) Mark has a rather interesting idea for the project.

8) The child spoke in a very soft voice.

9) What an amazingly simple test that was!

10) Your plan is certainly clever.

Activity B   Write on your paper the adverb that tells about the adjective in bold.

1) I am almost **ready** to go.

2) Fernando was rather **happy** today.

3) That coat is too **small** for you.

4) Ms. Edwards was quite **pleased** with the class.

5) They were completely **satisfied** with their new stove.

6) An extremely **strong** wind blew down the old oak tree.

7) That was a very **odd** thing for him to do.

8) She spoke in an unusually **soft** voice.

9) I'm not entirely **sure** of my plans.

10) Your puppy has so **much** energy!

Activity C   Write on your paper the adverb that tells about the adverb in bold.

1) Do your homework very **carefully**.

2) Alissa works too **quickly**.

3) The band played unusually **well**.

4) I am leaving sometime **today**.

5) He went far **away**.

6) Rita left much **later** than Donya.

7) Carlo swims rather **often**.

8) The children walked quite **slowly**.

9) Ellie gets up so **early** for work.

10) She tried awfully **hard** to win the race.

Activity D   Write these sentences on your own paper. Add an adverb of degree before the adjective or adverb in bold. Use a different adverb in each sentence.

1) The **strong** man lifted five hundred pounds.

2) Pedro is **ready**.

3) Your new sweater is **pretty**.

4) Rhoda does her work **well**.

5) Anne plays tennis **often**.

6) Lin works **quickly**.

7) Dana is **late**.

8) The bus arrived **early**.

9) We watched the **small** bug crawl across the table.

10) Mom is **happy** about her new job.

Activity E   Use each adverb of degree below in a sentence. Write the sentences on your paper.

1) very

2) too

3) quite

4) rather

5) somewhat

6) extremely

7) unusually

8) completely

9) so

10) almost

Part A   Write the adverbs of degree in these sentences on your paper.

1) Lou enjoyed his job at the bookstore very much.

2) Saturday was an unusually busy day.

3) Lou worked extremely hard.

4) Mrs. Marshall was completely satisfied with Lou's work.

5) "You are an exceptionally good worker," she told him.

6) "You can expect a very nice raise next month."

7) Lou was quite pleased to hear that!

8) The extra money would be so nice.

Part B   Write each of these sentences on your paper. Add an adverb of degree to tell about the adjective or adverb in bold in the sentence. Try to use a different adverb in each sentence.

1) December is a **cold** month.

2) People must dress **warmly**.

3) Many of the trees are **bare**.

4) The skies may be **cloudy**.

5) **Soon** we will have snow.

6) I will be ready to go shopping **tomorrow**.

7) The wind was **noisy** all night.

8) Reggie was **proud** of his accomplishment.

Never and *not* are adverbs of negation. A negative adverb means that the action will not happen or that the state of being is not present. The adverb *not* is often hidden in a contraction.

EXAMPLES   She is **never** home.

Carol is **not** at school today.

My brother **won't** eat his dinner. (will not)

They **didn't** find the book. (did not)

Remember that adverbs tell something about a verb, an adjective, or another adverb.

Activity A   Write these sentences on your paper. Circle the adverbs of negation.

1) There is not enough snow to ski.

2) Fernando couldn't find his pencil.

3) It was not his fault.

4) I have never met him.

5) They had never been there before.

6) Isn't that a beautiful painting?

7) She never answers the phone during dinner.

8) Susan would never quit her job.

9) The play didn't start on time.

10) Lynn has never been on an airplane.

Part A   Write the adverbs of negation in these sentences on your paper.

1) Nick won't be at play practice tonight.

2) He does not think he's good enough.

3) The director never praised Nick.

4) I can't think of anyone who would be better in that part.

5) He should never quit acting.

6) We mustn't let him quit.

Part B   Rewrite these sentences on your paper. Add an adverb of negation to each sentence.

Example   The weather is warm enough for swimming.

The weather is **not** warm enough for swimming.

1) Greg could swim across the pool.

2) I have seen Ruby.

3) Virgil goes to the beach.

4) I have time for lunch.

5) Our neighbors have been here before.

6) Yoko did find her book.

Sometimes people are not sure whether a word is an adjective or an adverb. Review the definitions of those two parts of speech.

An adjective describes a noun or pronoun.

> **EXAMPLES**
>
> Nancy is **tall**.
>
> The word *tall* describes *Nancy*.
>
> *Nancy* is a noun; therefore, *tall* is an adjective.

An adverb answers a question about a verb, an adjective, or another adverb in a sentence.

> **EXAMPLES**
>
> Nancy walked **outside**.
>
> The word *outside* tells where Nancy walked.
>
> *Walked* is a verb; therefore, *outside* is an adverb.

Activity A Write the words in bold on your paper. Beside each word, write whether it is an *adjective* or an *adverb*.

1) Larry is **late**.
2) He is **here**.
3) That house is **large**.
4) She works **hard**.
5) He is a **hard** worker.
6) Jack lives **here**.
7) **Today** we ran.
8) We arrived **late**.
9) They arrived **later**.
10) We looked **up**.
11) He runs **fast**.
12) He's a **fast** runner.
13) He is **fast**.
14) The answer is **clear**.
15) Speak **clearly**!
16) We practice **daily**.
17) Do **daily** exercises.
18) Let's leave **early**.
19) Is this the **early** show?
20) We **usually** eat at noon.

Many adverbs are made from adjectives by adding the ending *-ly*.

EXAMPLES	Adjectives	Adverbs
	The cloth is **soft**.	He sang **softly**.
	The candy is **sweet**.	She smiled **sweetly**.
	Carol looks **happy**.	Fernando laughed **happily**.

Activity B Write the words in bold on your paper. Beside each word, write whether it is an adjective or an adverb.

1) The sea was very **calm** today.

2) Donna walked **calmly** out of the room.

3) Between classes the halls were **quiet**.

4) The boy **quietly** watched the movie.

5) "This is an **extremely** difficult case," the lawyer said.

6) "This is an **extreme** case," the lawyer said.

7) My new puppy is always **hungry**.

8) The hikers ate lunch **hungrily**.

Sometimes an adverb is made from a noun by adding *-ly*.

EXAMPLES	Noun	Adverb
	May I have **part** of that?	He is **partly** finished.

Activity C Write the words in bold on your paper. Beside each word, write whether it is a noun or an adverb.

1) The books were in alphabetical **order**.

2) Please do things **orderly**.

3) We went to the store every **week**.

4) The family shops **weekly**.

5) The bills arrive every **month**.

6) We pay our bills **monthly**.

Not all words ending in *-ly* are adverbs. Many common adjectives end in *-ly*, too.

EXAMPLES	Dwayne received some **fatherly** advice from Mr. Belindo.
	Fatherly is an adjective that describes the noun *advice*.
	Janell is a **friendly** person.
	Friendly is an adjective that describes the noun *person*.

Other words that end in *-ly* may be used as adjectives or adverbs.

EXAMPLES	**Adjectives**	**Adverbs**
	He did the **daily** report.	He reported **daily**.
	We left in the **early** morning.	We left **early**.

Activity D   Write the words in bold on your paper. Beside each word, write whether it is an adjective or an adverb.

1) New cars are very **costly**.

2) **Only** Vanessa arrived on time.

3) That is an **ugly** cut.

4) They sat **quietly** and waited.

5) Donna's report was **timely**.

6) That is a **lovely** song.

7) Mr. Santos missed his **early** class.

8) They **easily** won first prize.

9) The car skidded **dangerously** close to us.

10) The music has a **lively** beat.

Part A   Write the words in bold on your paper. Beside each word, write whether it is an adverb or an adjective.

1) This **deadly** poison will get rid of all kinds of bugs.

2) Mr. Ozawa prepared his **yearly** report.

3) We receive a newspaper **daily**.

4) Please try to come to class **early**.

5) Carla smiled **happily**.

6) Where have you been **lately**?

7) I am **partly** finished with my report.

8) They went to Chicago on the **early** train.

9) We listened to the **daily** weather report.

10) The drought left the land bare and **ugly**.

Part B   Write two sentences for each of the words below on your paper. In the first sentence, use the word as an adjective. In the second sentence, use the word as an adverb.

1) fast

2) early

3) late

4) weekly

5) hard

6) inside

7) best

Many adverbs are used to make comparisons. The three degrees of comparison are positive, comparative, and superlative.

EXAMPLES	Positive	Comparative	Superlative
	fast	faster	fastest
	slowly	more slowly	most slowly
	happily	less happily	least happily
	well	better	best

One-syllable adverbs form their comparative and superlative forms by adding *-er* and *-est*. Adverbs of more than one syllable usually form their comparative and superlative forms by using *more* and *most*. Adverbs can also be compared with *less* and *least*. A few adverbs are irregular, such as *well, better,* and *best*.

Remember to use the comparative form to compare two things. Use the superlative form to compare more than two things.

EXAMPLES	Kim finished **more quickly** than Ben.
	Tom worked **most quickly** of them all.

Activity A   Write the adverbs in each of these sentences on your paper.

1) This shoe fits comfortably.

2) This shoe fits more comfortably than that one.

3) Of the three, that shoe fits most comfortably.

4) Victor is speaking calmly.

5) He is speaking more calmly than Hector.

6) He speaks most calmly when he has practiced his speech.

7) Jack writes well.

8) He writes better this year than last year.

9) He writes best about football.

Activity B   Write each adverb below on your paper. Beside each adverb, write its comparative and superlative forms.

Example   softly—**more softly, most softly**

1) loudly

2) brightly

3) fast

4) hard

5) gladly

6) clearly

7) softly

8) angrily

Activity C   Write the correct form of the adverb in parentheses to complete each sentence.

1) The lights shone (brightly) tonight than any night this week.

2) Liz sings (well) than Fernando.

3) Dan works (hard) when he is interested.

4) Of all the students, Kim worked (quickly).

5) Zeke played the trumpet (loudly) than his brother.

Part A Write the adverbs in each of these sentences on your paper. Beside each adverb, write the degree of comparison.

Example Sarah dances most unusually.

most unusually—superlative

1) Paul runs the mile faster than Sam.
2) Everyone in class worked hard.
3) I work best when I am rested.
4) Carl reads less quickly than Mike.
5) The choir sang the chorus more loudly than the verses.
6) Everyone worked least happily at the end of the day.
7) I like apples better than pears.
8) The winds howled most loudly at midnight.
9) The children played more quietly after lunch.
10) Irene plays the drums well.

Part B Write each adverb below on your paper. Beside each adverb, write its comparative and superlative forms.

Example quietly—**more quietly, most quietly**

1) happily
2) quickly
3) well
4) loudly
5) politely
6) sweetly
7) noisily
8) briskly
9) sadly
10) kindly

Adverbs often tell when the action in a sentence is taking place. *Ago* indicates past time. *Later* indicates future time. In a statement, the tense of the verb and the adverb of time usually must agree.

EXAMPLES Maria **sang** long **ago**.

Jack **will sing later**.

Tom **will sing next**.

(The adverb *next* suggests that the action will happen in the future. The verb should be in future tense.)

Tomorrow we **will go** to work.

(The adverb *tomorrow* is future time. The verb should be in future tense.)

Activity A   In the sentences below, the adverbs of time are in bold. Write the correct tense of the verb in parentheses to complete each sentence.

1) We (go) there a year **ago**.
2) **Yesterday** we (be) late to class.
3) Sally (arrive) **soon**.
4) Tiny (eat) his dinner **now**.

Always use an adverb in a sentence when answering a question about a verb.

EXAMPLES Correct: She sighed **softly**. (How did she sigh? *softly*)

Incorrect: She sighed **soft**. (*Soft* is an adjective.)

Activity B   Choose the correct word in parentheses. Write it on your own paper.

1) Fernando laughed (happy, happily).
2) The winds howled (loud, loudly).
3) She left home (quick, quickly)!
4) Sit there (quiet, quietly)!

Use *good* and *well* correctly. *Good* is always an adjective and describes a noun. Never use *good* to answer questions about a verb.

> **EXAMPLE**
>
> Correct: We had a **good** day. (What kind of day? a *good* day)
>
> Incorrect: They worked **good** together. (The adjective *good* should not be used to answer the question *How did they work?*)

Well is usually an adverb. *Well* means to do something correctly.

> **EXAMPLE**
>
> Correct: She speaks **well**. (How does she speak? *well*)
>
> Incorrect: She speaks **good**. (The adjective *good* should not be used to answer the question *How does she speak?*)

Good and *well* can both be used after state-of-being verbs. In both sentences below, *good* and *well* are adjectives.

> **EXAMPLE**
>
> Correct: I feel **good** today. (describes emotions)
>
> Correct: I feel **well** today. (describes health)

Activity C   Write either *good* or *well* on your paper to complete each sentence correctly.

1) Carol is _____ at arithmetic.
2) Dan dances very _____.
3) She did her _____ deed for the day.
4) Mike always does his work _____.
5) Paco isn't feeling _____ today.
6) Billy does everything _____.
7) Ellie paints very _____.
8) Michael had a _____ game yesterday.
9) Lulu sings very _____.
10) Do you feel _____ enough to go to the movies.

Part A Rewrite each of these sentences correctly on your paper.

1) Yesterday we are late to class.

2) Please finish that work quick.

3) Louis Armstrong played the trumpet very good.

4) Owen and I work good as partners.

5) "Julio spoke now," the teacher reminded the class.

6) Annie always talks very soft.

7) The phone works poor.

8) The children are playing so quiet.

9) Jonas dances good for a five-year-old.

10) The bus arrived soon.

Part B The word in bold in each of these sentences is an adverb. Write the form of the verb that should appear in each sentence to make it correct. Beside each verb, write its tense.

Example   I (sit) at that desk **yesterday**.

          sat—past tense

1) **Tomorrow** we (go) to work.

2) We (eat) at that restaurant a long time **ago**.

3) Our friends (arrive) **soon**.

4) The men (clean) our rug **yesterday**.

5) I (wash) the car **earlier today**.

Part A   Write all the adverbs in these sentences on your paper. A sentence may have more than one adverb.

1) A heavy snowfall arrived early in December.

2) Most of the people at Wilson High School were very happy.

3) The teachers and students waited somewhat patiently.

4) They were expecting an announcement that school would be dismissed early.

5) At home Joe was not so pleased.

6) He had to go to work anyway.

7) He knew the roads would be extremely slippery.

8) The grocery store never closed for snow.

9) Business at the store would probably be very slow.

10) Yesterday had been unusually busy for a Tuesday.

11) Joe drove more slowly that day.

12) Finally, he arrived at work.

13) He walked across the parking lot carefully.

14) The store was almost empty.

15) The other cashiers were talking excitedly about the snow.

16) The day passed quickly.

17) Soon it was time for Joe to leave.

18) "I still have time to go sledding," he thought to himself.

19) He found Tina already outside.

20) "Hey! I'm here!" he called to her.

Part B Write the adverbs in these sentences on your paper.

1) You should follow the directions carefully.

2) Clues to the puzzle are hidden everywhere.

3) The weather was very cold yesterday.

4) You are making too much noise.

5) I was almost asleep.

6) Julie threw her dog's old collar away today.

7) Is it true that it hardly rains in southern California?

8) The basement is quite damp this time of year.

9) He made a rather strange request.

10) She almost always arrives late.

Part C Write the form of the adverb that should appear in each sentence to make it correct.

1) Of all the girls, Donna runs (fast).

2) Charlie works (slowly) than Jim.

3) Beth sings well, but Dan sings (well).

4) When I am tired, I work (quickly) than when I am rested.

5) The cardinal sings (sweetly) than the blue jay.

Test Taking Tip Review your corrected tests. You can learn from previous mistakes.

Chapter

7

The Preposition

Suppose you are telling someone how you will be spending the evening. You might say, "I am going *to* the movies. A friend is coming *with* me." Words such as *to* and *with* show connection among words.

A preposition is a word that shows a relationship between a noun or pronoun and another word in the sentence. A preposition is the first word of a prepositional phrase. Prepositional phrases give information about ideas in sentences.

In Chapter 7, you will learn about prepositions, prepositional phrases, and their purposes. Each lesson in the chapter focuses on recognizing prepositions and their purpose in sentences. Knowing how prepositions work in a sentence will help you better understand relationships among ideas.

Goals for Learning

▶ To identify prepositions in sentences

▶ To identify prepositional phrases in sentences

▶ To distinguish between adjective and adverb phrases

▶ To distinguish between prepositions and adverbs

▶ To identify the correct form of pronouns used as objects of prepositions

Preposition

A word that shows how a noun or pronoun is related to another word in the sentence.

A **preposition** shows a relationship between a noun or a pronoun and another word in the sentence. The noun or pronoun that follows the preposition is called the object of the preposition.

The preposition, the object of the preposition, and any words in between make up a **prepositional phrase**.

EXAMPLES   Danzel gave his ticket **to Angie**. (The preposition *to* shows the relationship of *Angie*, the object of the preposition, to *gave*.)

Jan read the letter **from Mary**. (The preposition *from* shows the relationship of *Mary*, the object of the preposition, to *letter*.)

Prepositional phrase

A phrase that begins with a preposition and ends with a noun or a pronoun.

When the preposition changes, the relationship between the words in the sentence changes. Notice how the relationship between *spoke* and *Ben* changes in the following sentences.

EXAMPLES   Joseph spoke **to** Ben.

Joseph spoke **about** Ben.

Joseph spoke **for** Ben.

Here is a list of commonly used prepositions.

about	around	beneath	for	near	out	to
above	at	beside	from	of	over	under
across	before	down	in	off	past	until
after	behind	during	into	on	through	with

Activity A   Complete each of these sentences with a preposition. Write the complete sentence on your paper. More than one preposition may make sense in the sentence. Choose just one.

1) The apples _____ the tree are ripe.

2) The story _____ Edgar Allan Poe was written in 1838.

3) The girl _____ the picture is my sister.

4) The boots _____ the chair are mine.

5) The girl _____ Ken is a good dancer.

In a prepositional phrase, the preposition may have more than one object.

EXAMPLE Conchetta is friends with **Luke** and **Theo**.
(*Luke* and *Theo* is the compound object of the preposition *with*.)

In a prepositional phrase, the object of a preposition may have adjectives in front of it.

EXAMPLE across **the muddy** field

Because adverbs can answer questions about adjectives, a prepositional phrase may also contain an adverb.

EXAMPLE after the **very** long meeting

Usually when the object of the preposition is a pronoun, no other words are between the preposition and its object or objects.

EXAMPLES to him   beside it   between you and me

A sentence may have more than one prepositional phrase.

EXAMPLE We bought groceries **for supper at the store**.

Activity B Write the prepositional phrases in these sentences on your paper. Underline the preposition once and its object or objects twice. A sentence may have more than one prepositional phrase.

1) Write your name in the left-hand corner.

2) They live near a very busy highway.

3) Would you please sit on the bench with Sal and me?

4) Give this book about Mexico to him.

5) Early in the morning, the sun shines through the front window.

Activity C Write sentences for each of these prepositions on your paper.

Example   around—Her house is **around the corner**.

1) about   **4)** during   **7)** under   **10)** through

2) through   **5)** beside   **8)** in   **11)** behind

3) with   **6)** down   **9)** across   **12)** after

Compound prepositions are made up of more than one word.

EXAMPLES		
according to	in spite of	
because of	instead of	
in addition to	out of	
in front of	as far as	
in place of	along with	

Activity D Write the prepositional phrase in these sentences on your paper. Underline the compound preposition in each phrase.

Example   John stood in front of Maria.—<u>in front of</u> Maria

1) According to Jorge, the party was fun.

2) I am going instead of Tim.

3) Tranh will speak in place of Judy.

4) In spite of the heavy rain, they played the soccer game.

5) Donna sat in front of Karl.

6) Because of his bad cold, Abdul stayed home.

Part A   Write the prepositional phrases in these sentences on your paper. Underline the preposition once. Underline its object twice. A sentence may have more than one prepositional phrase.

1) My dog Honey was sleeping in the shade under a tree.

2) Suddenly, a loud noise in the street frightened her.

3) Honey ran around the yard wildly.

4) From the porch, I called her inside the house.

5) She dashed up the stairs instantly.

6) I almost fell onto my back when she jumped into my arms.

7) The noise had come from my neighbor's old car.

8) In spite of its age, the car still ran.

9) Mr. Kostas did have trouble starting the car during a rainstorm.

10) After a few tries, he could usually get it going.

Part B   Write all the prepositional phrases in these sentences on your paper. A sentence may have more than one prepositional phrase.

1) Emilio was studying for his final exams.

2) He stayed in his room and studied for several hours.

3) Cal called him on the telephone.

4) "I need some help from you with my math," he said.

5) Cal lived around the corner.

6) After a few minutes, he arrived in a panic.

7) He burst into Emilio's room.

8) "Please help me with these problems," Cal begged.

9) In addition to a math test, Cal had an English test the next day.

10) In spite of his worries, Cal passed both tests.

A prepositional phrase begins with a preposition and ends with a noun or a pronoun. A prepositional phrase may be used as an adjective phrase or as an adverb phrase.

An adjective is a word that describes or defines a noun or pronoun. A prepositional phrase used as an adjective does the same thing as an adjective. The phrase tells *which one, what kind,* or *how many.*

EXAMPLES   The house **across the street** was sold. (*Which house?* The one *across the street.*)

This book **by Judy Blume** is popular. (*Which book?* The one *by Judy Blume.*)

An adjective usually comes before the noun it describes. An adjective phrase always follows the noun it describes.

EXAMPLES   Adjective: The **Wilson High** team won.

Prepositional phrase: The team **from Wilson High** won.

Activity A   Write the adjective phrase in bold on your paper. Beside each phrase, write the noun or pronoun it describes.

Example   A friend **of mine** called.   **of mine—friend**

1) The boy **with me** is my cousin.
2) The flowers **on the table** are beautiful.
3) We built a house **of bricks and stone.**
4) None **of the girls** left early.
5) The poem **by Maya Angelou** was beautiful.

Activity B   Rewrite these sentences on your paper. Add an adjective phrase to describe the noun in bold. Be sure each phrase begins with a preposition.

1) The **story** was exciting to read.
2) Sue bought **tickets**.
3) Mom studied the **map**.
4) The **lamp** needed a new bulb.
5) The **house** looked empty.

An adjective phrase can describe the object of another preposition.

EXAMPLE	The man **at the end of the line** is Mr. Jones.
	The adjective phrase *at the end* describes the noun *man*; the adjective phrase *of the line* describes the noun *end*.

Activity C Write the adjective phrases in these sentences on your own paper. Beside each phrase, write the noun or pronoun it describes.

1) The woods beside the lake near our house are dark.

2) Elvin's dad owns a shoe store in the mall beside Jones River.

3) The woman with the baby in her arms is my aunt.

4) The lamp on the table beside your bed needs a new lightbulb.

5) All of the people in the auditorium cheered.

Activity D Rewrite these sentences on your paper. Add an adjective phrase after each noun or pronoun in bold.

1) **Everyone** enjoys the football **games**.

2) Several **friends** are coming to the **party**.

3) The **dish** fell from the **counter**.

4) The **man** bought a new **car**.

5) The **teacher** liked that **book**.

6) The **library** closed at **noon**.

Lesson Review Write the adjective phrases in these sentences on your paper. Beside each phrase, write the noun or pronoun it describes.

Example The pen on Frank's desk has no ink.

on Frank's desk—pen

1) January temperatures in Alaska are very cold.

2) The beautiful pines throughout the state are snow-covered.

3) Maria studied the history of Alaska.

4) Vitus Bering was the first explorer of Alaska.

5) People from Russia also explored Alaska.

6) Juneau, on the southeast coast, became Alaska's capital city.

7) Alaska became the largest state in the United States.

8) The population of Alaska is very small.

9) Alaska is one of our last frontiers.

10) My aunt from Washington State visited Alaska.

11) Her vacation cruise through Alaska's icy waters lasted fourteen days.

12) The picture on the postcard she sent us showed a glacier.

13) Aunt Rita visited Mendenhall Glacier near Juneau.

14) The massive glacier before her covered an entire valley.

15) Her stories about her cruise are exciting.

An adverb is a word that answers questions about a verb. A prepositional phrase used as an adverb does the same thing as an adverb. It answers the questions *How? When? Where?* and *How much?* or *How long?*

EXAMPLES	Adverb:	We shopped **rapidly**.
	Adverb phrases:	We shopped **in a hurry**. (*How did we shop? in a hurry*)

An adverb phrase may come anywhere in a sentence.

EXAMPLES   **After supper**, we napped.

We napped **after supper**.

Activity A   Write the adverb phrase in bold in these sentences on your paper. Beside each phrase, write the question that the adverb phrase answers about the verb. Write *How? When? Where? How Much?* or *How long?*

1) **For three hours**, the band played.
2) Maria ironed her dress **with great care**.
3) Dad slid the roast **into the oven**.
4) **Before midnight**, the report was written.
5) Write your paragraph **in ink**.
6) They stayed **about an hour**.

An adverb phrase can also answer the question *Why?* about a verb.

EXAMPLE   They were crying **because of the sad ending**. (*Why were they crying? because of the sad ending*)

Activity B   Write the adverb phrase that answers the question *Why?* in each of these sentences on your paper.

1) I ran inside because of the rain.
2) She shopped for dinner.
3) Will you sing for me?
4) Because of his fever, Jeff stayed home.

An adverb can describe an adjective or another adverb. An adverb phrase can do the same.

 EXAMPLES   Fred is now taller **by three inches**. (*Taller* is an adjective. The adverb phrase *by three inches* tells how much taller Fred is.)

In the race, Dan ran faster than Jack **by eight seconds**. (*Faster* is an adverb. The adverb phrase *by eight seconds* tells how much faster Dan ran.)

Activity C   Write the adverb phrases in these sentences on your paper. A sentence may have more than one adverb phrase.

1) Put the paper in the trash can.

2) His office is on the third floor in that tall building.

3) She shopped with her mother at the store.

4) Carol wrote for the school newspaper.

5) The firefighters saved the family from the fire.

6) Because of the weather, officials ended the game.

7) Tina is older than her sister by five minutes.

Activity D   Rewrite these sentences on your paper. Add an adverb phrase that answers *How? When? Where?* or *How much?* about the word in bold.

1) Zack **walks** every day.

2) They **arrived**.

3) Luisa **took** her coat.

4) Bob got the **highest** grade on the test.

5) The winds **blew** very hard.

6) Please **answer**.

Part A Write the adverb phrases in these sentences on your paper. A sentence may have more than one adverb phrase.

1) Marcus studies computer technology at Hanover Community College.

2) He will study there for two years.

3) Someday Marcus might work on computers in a bank.

4) During the early 1950s, the first computers were installed in business firms.

5) Now computers sit on office desks everywhere.

6) At school, Marcus learns about computer languages.

7) A computer programmer works with computer languages.

8) Because of the programmer's directions, the computer performs its job without a problem.

Part B Write whether the prepositional phrase in bold is an adjective or adverb phrase. Write your answers on your paper.

1) The letter **from Mary** arrived yesterday.

2) **At the concert**, the orchestra played the music **of Brahms**.

3) Both boys go **to Hanover Community College**.

4) Bess plays **for the Wilson High School soccer team**.

5) The gift **from my aunt** arrived **before my birthday**.

6) **During the winter** we enjoy skiing.

7) Honey chased a cat **up a tree**.

8) A girl **in my class** wrote a short story **about her summer vacation**.

9) She sent the story **to a magazine**.

10) The day **after tomorrow** is my birthday.

The object of the preposition is always a noun or a pronoun. Do not confuse a prepositional phrase with an infinitive, which begins with the word *to*. The word that follows *to* in an infinitive is a verb.

> **EXAMPLES**
>
> Infinitives: He wants **to leave** early.
> He hopes **to have** a job.
>
> Prepositional phrases: Chen went **to the bank**.
> Fran wrote a letter **to her aunt**.

Activity A Write on your paper whether the phrase in bold in these sentences is an *infinitive* or a *prepositional phrase*.

1) Marcus went **to his class**.

2) He likes **to work** with computers.

3) "Turn **to page 8**," the teacher said.

4) Marcus began **to read** his lesson.

5) He wanted **to ask** the teacher a question.

6) He went **to practice** on the computer.

7) Bill sent a get-well card **to his friend**.

8) The girl ran **to catch** the bus.

9) People on the bus waved **to her**.

10) Lynda climbed **to the top** of a high hill.

Activity B Write five sentences on your paper using the word *to*. Beside each sentence, write whether *to* introduces a prepositional phrase or an infinitive.

The object of the preposition is always a noun or a pronoun. If the object of a preposition is a pronoun, it must be in the objective case.

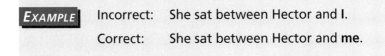

> **EXAMPLE**   Incorrect: She sat between Hector and **I**.
>
> Correct: She sat between Hector and **me**.

Possessive nouns and pronouns are NOT used as objects of prepositions.

> **EXAMPLE**   Incorrect: Roland went home with **his**.
>
> Correct: Roland went home with **him**.
>
> OR
>
> Roland went home with **his friend**.

Activity C   Write the prepositional phrases in these sentences on your paper. Underline the object of the preposition in each phrase.

1) Daria wanted to study with her friend.

2) The table was empty, so I put my books on it.

3) Patrick studied by himself.

4) We bought gifts for everyone.

5) They had to choose between them.

6) Marty asked, "May I have a salad with this?"

Activity D   Write these sentences on your paper. Correct any mistakes.

1) Please bring a coat for Pete and I.

2) Sam bought a soda for his.

3) Susan passed out papers to theirs.

4) Let's keep this secret between you and I.

The object of a preposition usually comes after the preposition. However, sometimes the preposition and its object are separated in sentences that ask questions.

> **EXAMPLE** Object   Preposition
> **What** did you do that **for**?

Activity E Write on your paper the prepositions and their objects in these sentences on your paper.

1) Whom are you talking about?

2) Whom are Dionne and Len with?

3) What is that book about?

4) What was she was thinking of?

Activity F Write all the prepositional phrases in this paragraph on your paper. Do **not** include the three infinitives that are in the paragraph.

Have you ever heard of Mary Lyon? She was a pioneer in the education of women. Mary Lyon was born in 1797. She died in 1849. She taught in schools in New Hampshire and in Massachusetts. In those days, only rich women could get a good education. She raised money to begin a school for middle-class women. In 1837, she opened a school in Massachusetts. The name of the school was Mount Holyoke. There women studied about mathematics, science, and Latin. Mary Lyon's only goal was to teach. She won the love of everyone through her work. Mary Lyon wanted to give women confidence in themselves.

Lesson Review   Write the prepositional phrases in these sentences on your paper.

1) Marcus would like to get a job in a bank or an accounting firm.

2) He likes to work with computers.

3) Marcus had to study for a test.

4) He studied with Anita and me.

5) The teacher gave the test to everyone.

6) The students had to concentrate hard on the questions.

7) They had prepared for the test all week.

8) Marcus made a mistake on his paper.

9) "What did I do that for?" he thought.

10) Finally, he was finished with the test.

11) He gave his paper to the teacher and breathed a sigh of relief.

12) Marcus waved good-bye to his friends and ran out the door.

13) The bus came early on Wednesdays, and he didn't want to miss it.

14) The bus driver waited for Marcus to get to the bus stop.

15) During the ride, Marcus took some time to think about the test.

Some words can be either a preposition or an adverb. A preposition always has an object. An adverb does not.

EXAMPLES	Adverb:	Gabriel climbed **aboard**. (*Aboard* is not followed by a noun or a pronoun.)
	Preposition:	Gabriel climbed **aboard** the boat. (*Aboard* relates its object, the noun *boat*, to the rest of the sentence.)

Activity A   Write the word in bold on your paper. Beside it write whether it is an *adverb* or a *preposition*.

1) Please come **in**.

2) Howard walked **in** the woods.

3) Turn the lights **off** when you leave.

4) Jane jumped **off** the stage.

5) I will come **by** later.

6) Sam lives **by** the lake.

7) Last night, Mike came **over**.

8) Honey jumped **over** the fence easily.

Activity B   Write these sentences on your paper. Add at least one prepositional phrase to each sentence to make it more interesting. Be sure to add only prepositional phrases.

Example   The boy arrived.

    The boy **from San Antonio** arrived **in the evening**.

1) My aunt wrote me a letter.

2) The principal spoke.

3) My neighbor bought a new car.

4) The quarterback threw the ball.

5) The crowd cheered.

Part A Write the word in bold on your paper. Beside it write whether it is an *adverb* or a *preposition*.

1) The dog sat **outside** and barked all afternoon.

2) Leave the package **outside** the door.

3) Haven't we met **before**?

4) The elephant disappeared **before** our eyes!

5) Quick! Come look **out** the window!

6) There was a crash of thunder and the lights went **out**.

7) Sit **down** and rest awhile.

8) The old car rumbled **down** the highway.

9) The houses **along** the coast were in danger during the storm.

10) I broke my leg and had to hobble **along** on crutches for six weeks.

Part B Write two sentences for each of these words on your paper. In the first sentence, use the word as a preposition. In the second sentence, use the word as an adverb.

1) in

2) on

3) below

4) around

5) about

6) up

7) underneath

8) inside

9) near

10) through

Part A   Write the prepositional phrase in bold in these sentences on your paper. Beside each prepositional phrase, write whether it is an *adjective phrase* or an *adverb phrase*.

1) The dress **in the window** is on sale.

2) The letter **from Aunt Vera** arrived yesterday.

3) Carol waited **for the mail**.

4) **In the spring** we will plant a garden.

5) I mowed the lawn **for my neighbor**.

6) Jiro traveled **across the country** last summer **in a bus**.

7) I put my homework assignment **for English class inside my book**.

8) **During the night**, seventeen inches **of snow** fell.

9) The painting **of your grandparents** is beautiful.

10) I did it **for their fiftieth anniversary party**.

Part B   Write all the prepositional phrases in these sentences on your paper.

1) Mike came to see me for a minute.

2) He arrived in a yellow sports car.

3) We invited him to stay for dinner.

4) Dad made pizza with his secret sauce.

5) After supper, we all helped clean up.

6) On Sunday, Mike will hike up Sugar Drop Mountain with Connie and me.

7) For a beginner, that's a good mountain to hike.

8) Some of the trails are steep.

9) Still, Mike should be able to make it to the top without a problem.

10) The weather woman on Channel 6 said Sunday would be a great day for outdoor fun.

Part C Write these sentences on your paper. Add at least one prepositional phrase to each one to make the sentence more interesting.

1) Everyone was happy.
2) The weather was good.
3) The family went out.
4) They came home.
5) The family was tired.
6) We rested.
7) Louis did his homework.
8) Laverne called.
9) The sun set and the moon appeared.
10) The sky became dark.

Part D Write these sentences on your paper. Correct any mistakes.

1) Nathan watched television with his.
2) Mario wrote a letter to I.
3) Between you and I there has always been trust.
4) Alex bought a present for.
5) On the bus, Mark sat behind Clay and she.

Test Taking Tip When taking a true/false test, read each statement carefully. Write *true* only when the statement is totally true. Write *false* if part or all of the statement is false.

Chapter

8

The Conjunction

A conjunction is like a bridge between two parts of a sentence. Words like *and, but,* and *for* connect words in a sentence. A conjunction can connect words, phrases, or ideas that do the same job in a sentence. Using conjunctions when you write and speak can help you write sentences that are smooth and easy to understand.

In Chapter 8, you will learn about conjunctions. Each lesson in the chapter focuses on recognizing and using different kinds of conjunctions in sentences.

Goals for Learning

▶ To identify conjunctions in sentences

▶ To write compound sentences using coordinating conjunctions

▶ To write complex sentences using subordinating conjunctions

▶ To write sentences using correlative conjunctions

Conjunction

A word that connects related words or groups of words.

A **conjunction** is a word that connects parts of a sentence. A conjunction can connect words, phrases, or ideas that are used in the same way.

There are three kinds of conjunctions: the *coordinating conjunction,* the *subordinating conjunction,* and the *correlative conjunction.*

Coordinating conjunction

A conjunction that connects words or groups of words that do the same job in a sentence.

A **coordinating conjunction** connects words, phrases, or sentences that do not depend on each other to make sense. The following are the seven coordinating conjunctions:

and	nor	so
but	or	yet
for		

EXAMPLES

Words:	Rich plays the guitar **and** the trumpet.
Phrases:	He ran around the corner **and** out of sight.
Ideas:	I'd like to help you, **but** I'm busy.

Activity A Write the coordinating conjunction in each of these sentences on your paper.

1) Eight and eight make sixteen.

2) All night the winds blew and the snow fell.

3) The referee blew her whistle and stopped the game.

4) He had little money, yet he walked into the room like a king.

5) The actor sang well, but he could not dance.

6) I will drink juice or milk.

7) There was nothing good on television, so I went for a walk.

8) I could not study, for I had a headache.

9) Lois isn't hungry, nor am I.

Activity B   Complete each sentence with a coordinating conjunction. Write the conjunctions on your paper.

1) I will have milk _____ water with my dinner.

2) Paco hits well, _____ he cannot throw a curve ball.

3) Vic tried hard _____ made the team.

4) Louisa studies hard, _____ she always has time for her friends.

5) After school we played CDs _____ relaxed.

6) John Adams _____ Thomas Jefferson were vice-presidents of the United States.

7) President Harry Truman was born in 1884 _____ died in 1972.

A coordinating conjunction may connect two or more complete ideas.

> **EXAMPLE**   I will drink juice. I will drink milk.
>
> I will drink juice **or** milk. (The coordinating conjunction *or* connects the two objects *juice* and *milk*. The words that are the same in both sentences are not repeated.)

Activity C   Use coordinating conjunctions to connect the related ideas in the following pairs of sentences. Write the new sentences on your paper. You may need to change the verb form.

1) Lena likes tacos. Andy likes tacos.

2) Lloyd plays football. Lloyd plays baseball.

3) Langston Hughes wrote short stories. Langston Hughes wrote poetry.

4) I grew tomatoes in my garden. I grew green beans in my garden.

5) Laura tried out for the basketball team. Her twin sister SueAnn tried out for the basketball team.

Use a comma to separate words or phrases in a series. A series is three or more words or phrases. Place the comma after each item in the series. Do not put a comma after the last item in the series.

> **EXAMPLES**   Lisa and Becky arrived late. (Only two people— do not use commas)
>
> Lisa, Becky, and Sue arrived late. (Three people—use commas)
>
> We planted flowers in the front, in the back, and on the sides of the house. (Three phrases— use commas)

Activity D   Write these sentences on your paper. Add commas only where they are needed. Circle the conjunctions.

1) We planted bushes trees and flowers around the house.

2) We planted tulips daffodils and petunias.

3) Later we washed up changed our clothes and went out to dinner.

4) I ordered a salad and milk.

5) My brother sister and mother ordered the soup.

6) After dinner we talked about going to a movie playing miniature golf or taking a walk around the lake.

Activity E   Use each of these conjunctions in a sentence. Write your sentences on your paper. Try to write at least two sentences that contain items in a series. Be sure to punctuate any items in a series correctly.

1) and

2) but

3) or

4) nor

5) yet

6) for

Two or more sentences joined with a conjunction usually need a punctuation mark. Use a comma to separate sentences joined with *and, but, nor, or, for, so,* or *yet.*

 EXAMPLES   Marco dug up the garden, **and** Leslie planted the seeds.

Our family loves spinach, **but** none of us likes beets.

Sentences that are very short often do not need a comma to separate them.

 EXAMPLES   We went out and then we went home.

She is tall and he is short.

When you join complete sentences with the following words, use a semicolon (;) in front of them and a comma (,) after them.

also	furthermore	nevertheless
accordingly	however	otherwise
besides	instead	therefore
consequently	moreover	

EXAMPLES   Lisa likes to play the piano; **however,** she doesn't like to practice.

Lance worked all day; **nevertheless,** he didn't finish.

The words *but* and *for* can be used either as conjunctions or as prepositions.

> **EXAMPLES**
>
> Conjunction: Becky feeds her puppy dog food, **but** he prefers steak!
>
> Preposition: No one was hungry **but** Rob.
>
> Conjunction: Randy brought the equipment, **for** he was the team manager.
>
> Preposition: We knew that he would work hard **for** the team.

Activity F Write these sentences on your paper. Punctuate them correctly.

1) Lisa must hurry otherwise she will be late.

2) We wanted to go shopping instead we stayed home.

3) After dinner Lisa read a book Marco did homework Mr. Martinez watched TV and Mrs. Martinez just relaxed.

4) Karl rode the bus to school but he walked home.

5) The storm blew down several trees furthermore it damaged some telephone lines.

6) Roberto was hungry for Italian food but his sister wanted Chinese food.

Activity G Write on your paper whether the word in bold is a *preposition* or a *conjunction*.

1) Paul played tennis well, **for** he practiced every day.

2) The new apartment was beautiful, **but** the rent was high.

3) Everyone liked the story **but** Yolanda.

4) The students cheered loudly **for** their team.

Lesson Review   Write these sentences on your paper. Circle the coordinating conjunctions. Add any missing punctuation.

1) A new girl moved to the town where Lisa and Becky live.

2) Her name is Antoinette but everyone calls her Toni.

3) Toni is hearing impaired but she reads lips and signs.

4) She learned sign language and lip reading at a special school for the hearing impaired.

5) Some people think all hearing-impaired people should learn to read lips and others think sign language is best.

6) Lisa and Becky wanted to learn sign language for they wanted to be able to communicate with Toni.

7) Toni explained that some signs stand for whole words and ideas but that not every word or idea has a sign.

8) Some words have to be spelled out letter by letter therefore they would have to learn the finger alphabet.

9) There are twenty-six hand symbols in the finger alphabet and each symbol stands for a letter of the alphabet.

10) Toni showed the girls how to form each letter with their fingers gave them a booklet that showed all the symbols and told them to practice every day.

11) Becky Lisa and their mom practiced signing together at the dinner table each evening.

12) Toni often came over so she was able to help them.

13) Soon they could use signs or finger spelling easily.

14) "Next, we will start learning signs for whole words and ideas," Toni told them.

15) Sign language helped Toni Becky and Lisa communicate furthermore it was fun to learn something new and useful.

Subordinating conjunction

A conjunction that connects a dependent clause with an independent clause in a sentence.

A **subordinating conjunction** connects an independent clause with a dependent clause. An independent clause expresses a complete idea. A dependent clause is a group of words that has a subject and a verb but does not express a complete idea. Since a dependent clause does not express a complete thought by itself, it cannot stand alone as a sentence. A dependent clause depends on the main, or independent, clause to make sense. Like adverbs, dependent clauses answer the questions *When? Where? Why?* and *How?*

> **EXAMPLE**
>
> | Subordinating conjunction: | **If** the rain stops, we can start practice. (The subordinating conjunction *if* connects the incomplete idea *if the rain stops* to the main clause *we can start practice*.) |
> | --- | --- |

A dependent clause may be found at the beginning or the end of a sentence. Use a comma after a dependent clause only when it is at the beginning of the sentence.

> **EXAMPLES**
>
> | Comma: | **Unless you hurry**, you won't finish. **After the party was over**, we went home. |
> | --- | --- |
> | No comma: | You won't finish **unless you hurry**. We went home **after the party was over**. |

Here is a list of some commonly used subordinating conjunctions:

after	in order that	when
although	since	whenever
as	so	where
because	unless	wherever
if	until	while

Activity A Write the dependent clause in each of these sentences on your paper. Circle the subordinating conjunctions.

1) If you want to play the piano better, you have to practice.

2) I plan to study until I finish.

3) Justin saved his money in order that he could go to college.

4) When Lisa gets here, we will leave.

5) They ate popcorn while they watched the movie.

Activity B Add an independent clause (a complete thought) to each of these dependent clauses to make sentences. Write the sentences on your paper.

1) Although we had just eaten breakfast,

2) Until the other team scored,

3) Because my mom is at work,

4) Since I flew on an airplane,

5) When I finish this book,

Activity C Add a dependent clause to each of these sentences. Write the new complete sentences on your paper. Circle the subordinating conjunctions. Add commas where needed.

1) Dan would like to visit California.

2) Darryl saved twenty-five dollars a week.

3) My neighbors asked me to water their garden.

4) Anne's report was late.

5) Marcus went to the new computer store.

6) The storm forced people to stay home.

7) Cassie watched a nature program about crocodiles.

8) A strange noise woke me up from a deep sleep.

9) Lee left his school books at the library.

10) The front door slammed shut.

Activity D Connect each of these pairs of sentences with a subordinating conjunction. Write the new complete sentences on your paper. Add commas where needed.

1) Zack is lifting weights. He wants to be on the wrestling team.

2) Pete went to the library. He needed a book.

3) Tina moved to town in March. She has been in Becky's English class.

4) I was asleep. A storm blew down our tree.

5) You will drive today. I will drive tomorrow.

6) Jan wants to see that play. We will buy tickets ahead of time.

7) The baseball team won the championship. The town celebrated.

8) Tom walked into the room. Everyone began to clap.

9) The sun set. We walked around the lake.

10) I am drying the dishes. You can pick out a movie.

Some words can be used either as subordinating conjunctions or as prepositions.

> **EXAMPLES** Conjunction: The game was put off **until** the rain stopped. (*Until the rain stopped* is a dependent clause that is connected to the main clause by the subordinating conjunction *until*.)
>
> Preposition: The game was put off **until** tomorrow. (*Until tomorrow* is a prepositional phrase introduced by the preposition *until*. Remember that prepositional phrases never include verbs.)

Activity E Write on your paper whether the word in bold is a *conjunction* or a *preposition*.

1) Donna went home **after** school.

2) We went home **after** school was over.

3) **Because of** Marco, we won the game.

4) I like that coat **because** it is warm.

5) I haven't heard from her **since** Monday.

6) I'll leave **since** you are here now.

7) **Before** class began, I talked to the teacher.

8) **Before** lunch, I have Spanish class.

Activity F Write the subordinating conjunctions in each of these sentences on your paper.

1) We drove home carefully because it was snowing.

2) We had classes until noon although the weather was bad.

3) If the snow is deep enough, there will be no school tomorrow.

4) School is closed only when the snow is deep.

5) Where Lisa and Marco live, there are usually two deep snows each year.

Part A Write these sentences on your paper, adding commas where needed. Circle the subordinating conjunctions in each sentence.

1) Kathy will hold dinner until everyone gets here.

2) If you will help we can finish early.

3) When warm weather arrives Marco and Anthony will go fishing.

4) Until the team scored the fans were quiet.

5) Everyone cheered as the band began playing the school song.

6) I took the bus because I was late.

7) Whenever I hear that song I think about my grandmother.

8) Since we finished our homework early let's watch a movie.

9) We will plant a vegetable garden after the ground thaws.

10) As the clock struck ten I became sleepy.

Part B Connect each of these pairs of sentences with a subordinating conjunction. Write the new sentences on your paper. Add commas where needed. Be sure the sentences make sense.

1) Mai got an excellent grade on her test. She studied hard.

2) I will clean the house. You do the shopping.

3) Jon got hungry about three o'clock. He ate an apple.

4) The weather is too cold. I can't go outside.

5) He lost the election. He didn't have enough help.

6) They waited for the bus. Tommy and Steve went over their notes.

7) The sun was shining. There was a cold, raw wind.

8) Gloria looked all over the house. She found her math book.

9) I get near fresh flowers. I begin to cough.

10) You may not make it to the bank. It closes at three.

Correlative conjunctions

A pair of conjunctions that connects words or groups of words that are related.

Correlative conjunctions express a shared relationship and are always used in pairs.

EXAMPLES	**Neither** Marco **nor** Anthony enjoyed that movie.
	Both the actors **and** the story were weak.

Here is a list of the most common pairs of correlative conjunctions:

both	and
either	or
neither	nor
not only	but also
whether	or

Activity A   Write the correlative conjunctions in each of these sentences on your paper.

1) Ann Marie will write her report on either James Polk or Benjamin Harrison.

2) Both Polk and Harrison were presidents of the United States.

3) Not only Ann Marie but also Susan must write a report.

4) Neither Polk nor Harrison is very famous.

5) Susan doesn't know whether to write about Chester Arthur or Franklin Pierce.

6) She had heard of neither Arthur nor Pierce before.

When subjects are joined with correlative conjunctions, the verb usually agrees with the subject nearer the verb.

EXAMPLES

Incorrect:	**Neither** Justin **nor** Mark are home yet.
Correct:	**Neither** Justin **nor** Mark is home yet. (*Mark* is singular.)
Incorrect:	**Not only** the house **but also** the garage need painting.
Correct:	**Not only** the house **but also** the garage needs painting. (*Garage* is singular.)
Incorrect:	**Either** candy **or** flowers is a nice gift.
Correct:	**Either** candy **or** flowers are a nice gift. (*Flowers* is plural.)

However, when subjects are joined by *and*, the verb always takes the plural form.

EXAMPLE

Incorrect:	**Both** Karla **and** Joe takes piano lessons.
Correct:	**Both** Karla **and** Joe take piano lessons.

Activity B   Write the words that should appear in each sentence to make it correct.

1) Either a pencil or a pen (is, are) all right to use.

2) Neither the coat nor the shoes (is, are) on sale.

3) Neither the car nor the truck (is, are) working today.

4) Either perfume or flowers (makes, make) a nice gift for your aunt's birthday.

5) If I'm right, either your photographs or his sculpture (have, has) received an award.

6) Both Yvette and her sister (loves, love) cooking.

Part A   Write the correlative conjunctions in each of these sentences on your paper.

1) The football team scored not only the touchdown but also the extra point.

2) Would you like either milk or juice?

3) Both Chandra and her sister speak three languages.

4) She bought neither the dress nor the suit.

5) Either school will start late or it will be canceled.

6) Carol likes neither ice hockey nor football.

7) Either milk or juice will be fine.

8) For my birthday I got not only skis but also ski poles.

9) Alice didn't know whether to laugh or cry.

10) Kate, Inez, and Dwight are not only in the same homeroom, but they are also in all the same classes.

11) We could not decide whether to eat before the movie or after.

12) The gift was for both Julie and me.

13) Either try harder or don't play.

Part B   Complete these sentences with correlative conjunctions. Write the complete sentences on your own paper. There may be more than one correct answer.

1) _____ Mark _____ Justin have part-time jobs.

2) Susan thinks _____ the jeans _____ the shirt fit her right.

3) _____ Estelle _____ her brother is a talented artist.

4) Mr. Morales _____ drives to work _____ takes the bus.

5) Mrs. Brooks must learn _____ the reports _____ just the outlines are due on Monday.

Part A   Write all the conjunctions in these sentences on your paper.

1) Lisa and Tamara were making plans for the Spring Festival dance.

2) Tamara wondered whether Liang or José would ask her.

3) She decided to buy a new dress when she got paid.

4) Lisa wanted to ask Anthony, but she wasn't sure if he would go.

5) She didn't want to embarrass him if he didn't want to go with her.

6) After a few days passed, Lisa decided to ask Anthony.

7) "Either he'll agree to go or he won't," she thought.

8) Anthony did want to go, but first he had to talk to his boss.

9) "I either have to find someone else to work for me, or I'll have to work," he said.

10) Although he had to ask six different people, Anthony finally found someone to work for him.

Part B   Rewrite these sentences on your paper. Use a conjunction to connect the ideas.

1) Paul bought a coat. He bought a scarf. He bought some gloves.

2) It rained on Monday. It rained on Tuesday.

3) Dan was absent. Abby was absent.

4) Anthony asked his brother. Anthony asked his cousin Rick. Anthony asked two other friends.

5) Lisa would have a good time. She and Anthony have fun together.

Part C   Write these sentences on your paper. Add punctuation where needed.

1) Lisa Anthony Tamara and Liang went to the dance together.
2) Because the night was warm they put the top down on the car.
3) While they were on their way they listened to the radio and talked.
4) "If we don't get there soon we will miss the first dance," Tamara said.
5) "The dance committee wanted a band however they got a disc jockey," Lisa said.
6) When they arrived they hurried to join their friends.
7) "Shall we dance or shall we check out the food," Anthony asked.
8) "Unless you're hungry let's dance," she answered.
9) The music was good and they had a wonderful evening.
10) After the dance they went to a restaurant.

Part D   Complete these sentences with conjunctions. Write the completed sentences on your paper. There may be more than one correct answer.

1) They were hungry, _____ they were not tired.
2) _____ Liang _____ Anthony ordered hamburgers.
3) Lisa wanted something healthy _____ she ordered spinach salad.
4) _____ they were eating, the disc jockey from the dance came into the restaurant.
5) They talked about the dance, _____ soon it was time to go home.

Test Taking Tip   Prepare for a test by making a set of flashcards. Write a word on the front of each card. Write the definition on the back. Use the flashcards in a game to test your knowledge.

The Interjection

You often use words such as ***Oh no!*** or ***Wow!*** when you are cheering for your favorite team. Words such as *oh no* and *wow* express your excitement.

An interjection is a word or phrase that expresses strong feeling. While an interjection adds interest to a sentence, it is not necessary to the meaning of the sentence.

In Chapter 9, you will learn more about recognizing and using interjections in sentences.

Goals for Learning

▶ To use interjections in sentences

▶ To write sentences that contain an interjection

▶ To punctuate sentences that contain interjections correctly

Interjection

A word or phrase that shows strong feeling.

An **interjection** is a word or phrase that expresses a strong feeling. Always separate the interjection from the rest of the sentence with a punctuation mark. Use a comma, a question mark, or an exclamation point. Use an exclamation point after a strong interjection.

EXAMPLES

Hurry! I'll be late again.

Oh? I didn't know you were sick.

Hush! Everyone is working.

Say, could you help me?

Here are some other commonly used interjections:

ah	ouch
alas	quick
gosh	really
ha	sorry
hello	so what
hey	well
hurry	what
my goodness	whew
nonsense	wow
oh, boy	yes

When a period, a question mark, or an exclamation point follows an interjection, capitalize the first word of the sentence.

EXAMPLES

So? Who wants to take a break?

Wow! That is lovely.

Whew! I'm glad I am finished!

Do not capitalize the first word of the sentence that follows the comma after an interjection.

EXAMPLE   Ah, that dessert looks great!

Activity A   Rewrite these sentences on your paper. Add punctuation after the interjections and at the ends of the sentences. Capitalize the first words of sentences.

1) quick I need help fast

2) wow what a great car that is

3) really I didn't know that

4) well you finally got here

5) whew that was hard

Activity B   Write ten sentences that use interjections on your paper. Be sure to punctuate each sentence correctly.

Part A Add an interjection to each of these sentences. Write the new sentences on your paper. Be sure to punctuate correctly.

1) Isn't that beautiful?

2) We're having a test.

3) That hurts.

4) I ripped my best shirt.

5) I won!

6) What a sad story that was.

7) We left just in time!

8) You made it!

9) That can't be the right answer.

10) That sure smells great.

Part B Write these sentences on your paper. Punctuate and capitalize each sentence correctly.

1) no I can't help you

2) ouch that hurts

3) whew that has a strong smell

4) well what's new

5) hey I had better get home

6) alas she could not make it to the finish line

7) hurry I hear the train coming

8) honestly you would think they would behave

9) yikes a snake just crawled over Pam's foot

10) gosh this town looks deserted

Part C Complete each sentence with an interjection. Write the sentences on your paper. Punctuate and capitalize each sentence correctly.

1) _____ what a flop that play was

2) _____ you can't be serious

3) _____ that is a wonderful idea

4) _____ I burned my hand on that pot

5) _____ where did you learn to sing like that

6) _____ call the fire department

7) _____ do you mean it

8) _____ no one is going to believe this story

9) _____ was he angry

10) _____ we'll miss the bus

Part D Write 10 sentences using interjections. Be sure to capitalize and punctuate the sentences correctly.

Test Taking Tip When studying for a test, use a marker to highlight important facts and terms in your notes. For a final review, read over highlighted areas.

Sentence Construction

Y ou may have noticed that not every sentence has the parts of speech in the same order. A sentence must express a complete thought. It can, however, follow many different patterns to express that thought.

You may also have noticed that not every sentence has the same purpose. Sentences can have different purposes.

Statement	This kind of sentence states a fact or tells about something.
Question	This kind of sentence asks a question.
Command	This kind of sentence gives an order or makes a request.
Strong Feelings	This kind of sentence shows surprise or other strong feelings.

While every sentence must have certain parts to express a complete thought, those parts can be arranged and combined in different ways. There are four basic sentence structures.

Simple	One subject and one predicate
Compound	Two or more ideas joined with a conjunction
Complex	One independent and one dependent clause
Compound-Complex	At least two independent clauses and at least one dependent clause

In Part 2 of this book, you will learn about the different patterns that sentences follow and the different purposes sentences have. You will learn how to capitalize and punctuate sentences so that their purpose is clear. You will learn how to recognize the parts of a sentence. You will also learn how to put these parts together to express a complete thought.

When you know how to construct a sentence, you will be able to speak and write clearly. You will be able to express your ideas and communicate them to others. This is the real purpose of studying grammar.

Chapter
10

Sentences: Subjects and Predicates

When you tell a story, you express complete ideas so that listeners can picture the characters in the story and what happens to them. You break the ideas in your story into units of meaning called sentences.

A sentence is a group of words that expresses a complete thought. Every sentence has two parts. They are the subject and the predicate. The subject of a sentence is who or what the sentence is about. The predicate tells what the subject did or what happened to the subject.

Each lesson in Chapter 10 focuses on what a sentence is and how subjects and predicates work in different types of sentences.

Goals for Learning

▶ To identify a sentence

▶ To identify the subject and predicate in simple sentences

▶ To identify the noun or pronoun in subjects

▶ To identify the verb or verb phrase in predicates

▶ To identify different types of sentences

▶ To identify the subject and predicate in compound sentences

Sentence

A group of words that expresses a complete thought. A sentence always begins with a capital letter and ends with a period, question mark, or exclamation point.

A **sentence** is a group of words that expresses a complete thought. Every sentence begins with a capital letter and ends with a punctuation mark.

EXAMPLES

Mrs. Johnson sold her old car to Rafael.

What did he pay for the car?

Stop right there!

A group of words may look like a sentence, but if it does not express a complete thought, it is not a sentence.

EXAMPLES

Not a sentence:	The car with the red top. (This group of words does not express a complete thought. What about the car with the red top?)
Sentence:	The car with the red top belongs to her friend.
Not a sentence:	Looked all over town for a car. (This group of words does not express a complete thought. Who looked all over town for a car?)
Sentence:	Rafael looked all over town for a car.
Not a sentence:	Before Rafael bought the car. (This group of words does not express a complete thought. What happened before Rafael bought the car?)
Sentence:	Before Rafael bought the car, his father looked it over.

Activity A   For each item below, write *S* on your paper if the group of words is a sentence. Write *NS* if the group of words is not a sentence.

1) Stop for the red light!

2) Before the storm was over.

3) In the house across the street.

4) That's nice.

5) Where does she live?

6) Searching for a new job.

7) She laughed.

8) Jack went fishing.

9) Because of the cold weather.

10) Each day before the sun rises.

11) You can leave now.

12) Everyone at the party had a good time.

13) Chen moved to town in March.

14) On the day of the party for Mrs. Williams.

15) Afterwards, they all helped clean up.

Activity B   Copy each group of words from Activity A that you marked *NS* onto your paper. Add words to each item to make it a complete sentence. Check that each sentence begins with a capital letter and ends with a period, question mark, or exclamation point.

Part A For each item below, write *S* on your paper if the group of words is a sentence. If the group of words is not a sentence, copy it onto your paper and add words to make a complete sentence.

1) Our neighbor in the house across the street.

2) They painted the house a light shade of brown.

3) His whole family picked out the color.

4) They needed a two-story ladder.

5) When dark clouds appeared in the sky.

6) The part of the house under the roof.

7) The whole job took them three days.

8) After they were finished.

9) Feeling good about themselves.

10) Professional painters could not have done a better job.

Part B Copy each of the following groups of words onto your paper. Add words to make each one a complete sentence. Be sure to begin each sentence with a capital letter and end with a period, question mark, or exclamation point.

1) the papers on my desk

2) seen in the woods near the lake

3) walking to the game with friends

4) the girl on the bus

5) if anyone calls while I'm out

Subject

Who or what the sentence is about.

Every sentence has two parts: the **subject** and the predicate. The subject is the part of the sentence that tells what is being talked about. The main word in a subject is usually a noun or pronoun. The noun or pronoun and all the words that describe it make up the **complete subject**. The complete subject may be one word or many words.

Complete subject

All the words in the subject. It may be one word or many words.

EXAMPLES   **He** opened his book. (Who opened the book? *He* opened it.)

The woman who taught us Spanish last year became vice-principal. (Who became vice-principal? *The woman who taught us Spanish last year* did.)

Simple subject

The main noun or pronoun in the subject.

The **simple subject** is the main noun or pronoun in the complete subject.

EXAMPLES   The **quiz** on Friday was easy. (The simple subject is the noun *quiz*. The complete subject is *the quiz on Friday*.)

Mrs. Castillo is our Spanish teacher this year. (The simple subject is the proper noun *Mrs. Castillo*. The complete subject is also *Mrs. Castillo*.)

Activity A   Write the complete subject of each of these sentences on your paper. Circle the simple subject. A complete subject may be only one word.

1) Mrs. Castillo comes from Mexico City, Mexico.

2) The entire class speaks in Spanish every day.

3) The teacher asks the students questions in Spanish.

4) They must answer her in Spanish.

5) The students in this class learn quickly.

6) Our book has beautiful photographs of South America.

The simple subject cannot be the object of the preposition.

> **EXAMPLES**   **One** of the girls was late.
>
> (*One of the girls* is the complete subject. The prepositional phrase *of the girls* describes the simple subject *one*. *Girls* is the object of the preposition *of*; therefore, *girls* cannot be the subject of the sentence.)
>
> The **person** beside Carol is my aunt.
>
> (*The person beside Carol* is the complete subject. The prepositional phrase *beside Carol* describes the simple subject *person*. *Carol* is the object of the preposition *beside*; therefore, *Carol* cannot be the subject of the sentence.)

Activity B   The complete subject in each of these sentences is in bold. Write each simple subject on your paper.

1) **Each of the students** wrote the answer on his paper.

2) **All of my friends** like music.

3) **Eight of the students** were absent yesterday.

4) **The secretary in the principal's office** has the flu.

5) **Two of the students** had a fever.

Activity C   Write the complete subject in each of these sentences on your paper.

1) I am going to the store.

2) A friend of Mrs. Castillo visited from Spain.

3) Three of our classmates went on the field trip.

4) The car with the flat tire pulled off the road.

5) Everyone in the band practiced for the concert.

The subject of a sentence usually comes before the verb, but it may come after the verb. When a sentence begins with the words *here* or *there*, the subject comes after the verb.

EXAMPLES   There will be a **bus** at eleven-thirty. (What will be there? A *bus* will be there.)

Here comes **Amy** now. (Who comes now? *Amy* does.)

Activity D Write the simple subject in each of these sentences on your paper.

1) There is a good program on TV tonight.

2) Here is the bus stop.

3) There are no sandwiches left.

In a question, the subject may come between a helping verb and a main verb or the parts of a verb phrase.

EXAMPLES   When does **Mary** have math? (The subject *Mary* comes between the helping verb *does* and the main verb *have.)*

Are **you** leaving soon? (The subject *you* comes between the verb phrase *are leaving*.)

When the interrogative pronouns *what, who,* and *which* begin a sentence that asks a question, the interrogative pronoun may be the subject.

EXAMPLES   **Who** called?

What is happening?

Which of these books is yours?

Activity E Write the simple subject in each of these sentences on your paper.

1) Will you be going to the meeting?

2) Which of the members will speak?

3) Who will lead the discussion?

4) Has this group ever met before?

In a command or a request, the subject is *you*, even though the word *you* may not appear in the sentence. The subject is understood to be the person spoken to.

> **EXAMPLES** Please help me set the table.
>
> **(You)** Please help me set the table.
>
> Jack, come here right now.
>
> Jack, **(you)** come here right now. (Although the person spoken to is named, the subject is still understood to be *you*.)

Activity F   Write the simple subject in each of these sentences on your paper.

1) Pedro, help me carry these bags into the house.

2) Open your books to page 45.

3) Denise, please come home right after school.

4) Don't touch that!

5) Please hurry!

The subject of a sentence can be compound (two subjects).

> **EXAMPLES** **Connie** and **Brenda** went to class.
>
> The **girl** and her **friend** went shopping.

Activity G   Write the compound subject in each of these sentences on your paper.

1) Neither Freddie nor Tricia went to the concert.

2) Both my hat and my gloves were lost.

3) Spring and summer are my favorite seasons.

4) Are my books or my papers in your locker?

5) There are enough sandwiches and juice for everyone.

Part A Write the simple subject in each of these sentences on your paper. The subject may be understood.

1) Christa wanted a CD player.

2) On Saturday she looked at them in the store.

3) Her birthday was in two weeks.

4) Her mother talked to Christa's brother.

5) "Would Christa like anything special for her birthday?"

6) "Get her a CD player."

7) Who is coming to Christa's party?

Part B Write each of these sentences on your paper. Underline the complete subject. Then circle the simple subject.

1) Baseball season begins soon.

2) Is James on the team?

3) He usually plays first base.

4) There will be a tryout on Friday.

5) Where will tryouts be held?

6) José and Andy play baseball.

7) The state college had a good team last year.

8) Many of their best players have graduated.

9) Here are the names of some players still on the team.

Predicate

The part of a sentence that tells something about the subject.

The **predicate** of a sentence tells what the subject did or what happened to the subject. The predicate always includes a verb.

The **complete predicate** includes the main verb and all of the words that tell something about the verb. The complete predicate may be one word or many words. Any words in a sentence that are not part of the complete subject are part of the complete predicate.

Complete predicate

The part of a sentence that contains the main verb and all the words that describe the verb. The main word in the complete predicate is the verb or verb phrase.

EXAMPLES   We **studied**.

Andy **will look at new cars this weekend**.

Activity A   Write the complete predicate in each of these sentences on your paper.

1) Lena lost her earring yesterday.
2) Denise found the earring today.
3) One of the stones was missing.
4) Someone had apparently stepped on it.

The main part of the complete predicate is the verb or verb phrase. The verb or verb phrase in the complete predicate is sometimes called the simple predicate.

EXAMPLES   James *helped* **his father in the garage**. (The main word in the complete predicate is the verb *helped*.)

Anita *will meet* **us at the library**. (The main words in the complete predicate form the verb phrase *will meet*.)

Activity B   Write the complete predicate in each of these sentences on your paper. Underline the verb or verb phrase.

1) Mrs. Barry gave Christa a surprise birthday party.
2) Christa's brother Will baked a carrot cake.
3) Her friends had decorated the house.
4) Christa was arriving home at six thirty.

Usually the predicate part of the sentence comes after the subject.

 EXAMPLE The whole family **enjoyed the party**.

In a question, part of the complete predicate often comes before the subject.

EXAMPLES **Did** you **bring Christa a present**?

Where did you **buy it**?

Are you **having fun**?

Adverbs and prepositional phrases that are part of the complete predicate may be at the beginning of the sentence.

EXAMPLES **At eleven o'clock** everyone **went home**.

Then Will **helped his parents clean up**.

Activity C   Write the complete predicate in each of these sentences on your paper. Underline the verb or verb phrase.

1) Did you talk to Christa after the party?

2) Why did Elena leave early?

3) Maybe she was feeling sick.

4) After the party, Christa called Elena.

5) What was wrong?

6) Her mother needed her at home.

7) At the last minute, Mrs. Grasso was called in to work.

8) Elena babysits for her mother.

9) Usually, Mrs. Grasso does not work on weekends.

10) Because of a computer problem, she was needed in the office.

11) Luckily for Elena, the party was almost over.

The verbs in the predicate part of the sentence can be compound. A compound verb is made up of one or more verbs that are joined by a conjunction such as *and, but,* or *or.* Compound verbs share the same subject.

EXAMPLES   The sun **moved** behind the cloud and **disappeared**.

The audience **clapped** and **cheered**.

They **looked** calm but **were** very nervous.

Activity D   Write the complete predicate in each of these sentences on your paper. Underline the verb or verbs in the predicate.

1) Andy looked at new cars but did not buy one.

2) The big cars cost too much and used too much gas.

3) The small cars got good gas mileage but remained out of his price range.

4) The used cars showed rust spots and needed repairs.

5) Should he buy that car or look some more?

6) He thought about it but could not decide.

7) His parents talked to him and gave him some advice.

8) He would save some more money and look again in the spring.

Activity E   Write five sentences with compound verbs in the predicate on your paper. Circle each verb or verb phrase in your sentences.

Part A Write these sentences on your paper. Underline the complete predicate in each sentence.

Examples   Do you <u>like apples</u>?

On Sunday, we <u>will pick apples</u>.

You <u>can pick from the bottom branches or use the ladder</u>.

1) Will you come to our apple picking party this Sunday?
2) When does it start?
3) Around two o'clock, all of my relatives will arrive.
4) Usually, they talk for a while and then climb back into their cars.
5) The apple orchard is not far from our house.
6) We will walk around the orchard and pick apples.
7) Then everyone will return to my house for a huge fall dinner.
8) Can I bring anything?
9) Bring a big appetite!

Part B Write each of these sentences on your paper. Underline the complete predicate. Then circle each main verb or verb phrase.

1) In the spring, people think about outdoor activities.
2) Some of the neighbors are planting flowers.
3) I always know the first day of spring.
4) My neighbor Matt takes his fishing gear out.
5) Usually, he is out in his yard with his fishing rod.
6) He cleans his gear and practices his casting.
7) Every year, he goes on a fishing vacation.
8) He dreams about catching the big one.
9) Last year it got away.
10) Will this year be different?
11) He has already invited us to a fish dinner.

Every sentence has a purpose. A sentence can make a statement. A sentence can ask a question. A sentence can give a command or make a request. A sentence can show strong feelings.

EXAMPLES	Statement:	They went to the concert.
	Question:	Are you going to the concert?
	Command:	Go to the concert with them.
	Strong feeling:	What a great concert that was!

A sentence that makes a statement usually begins with the subject. A statement ends with a period.

EXAMPLE	The **concert** began at eight o'clock.

A sentence that asks a question begins with either a helping verb or an interrogative pronoun or adverb. A question ends with a question mark.

EXAMPLES	**Are** you ready yet?	**Who** is she?
	Did you like the music?	**Where** are my shoes?

A sentence that makes a command or request begins with a verb. The subject is understood to be the person spoken to. A command usually ends with a period. A strong command may end with an exclamation mark.

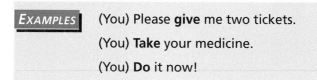

EXAMPLES	(You) Please **give** me two tickets.
	(You) **Take** your medicine.
	(You) **Do** it now!

A sentence that shows strong feeling or excitement ends with an exclamation mark.

> **EXAMPLES**   I can't believe our team won!
>
> What a great game that was!

Activity A   Decide the purpose of each of these sentences. Write *S* on your paper if the sentence makes a statement. Write *Q* if the sentence asks a question. Write *C* if the sentence makes a command or request. Write *SF* if the sentence shows strong feelings or excitement.

1) Are you hungry?

2) I am starved!

3) We can eat at this restaurant.

4) Melissa and her parents had lunch here last week.

5) Do you know what you want?

6) Please order something for both of us.

7) I'm having the soup and sandwich special.

8) That sounds good to me.

9) What kind of sandwich would you like?

10) Decide quickly!

11) I'll have the tuna on dark rye.

12) Here is your check.

13) Has someone made a mistake?

14) This can't be the right amount!

15) Next time, we'll eat at my house.

Part A   Write the following sentences on your paper. Add correct end marks. Beside each sentence, write its purpose (*Statement, Question, Command or Request, Strong Feeling*).

Example   Jump now
              Jump now!—Command

1) Listen to this new CD

2) What a terrific sound that is

3) Where do you buy your CDs

4) The music store at Crosstown Mall has the best prices

5) What is the average price of a tape or CD at the store near school

6) Look at the ad in the paper

7) That ad lists the prices of the most popular CDs

8) These must be the highest prices in town

9) Don't ever shop there

10) I won't

Part B   Write an example of each kind of sentence listed below on your paper. Be sure to begin each sentence with a capital letter and end it with the correct mark.

1) a statement

2) a question

3) a command

4) a strong command

5) a request

6) a sentence that shows strong feeling or excitement

Simple sentence

A sentence that has one subject and one predicate and expresses a complete idea.

A **simple sentence** has one subject and one predicate. A simple sentence is an **independent clause**, or a sentence that expresses a complete thought.

A **compound sentence** has two or more independent clauses joined together with a conjunction. Each clause has a subject and a predicate and expresses a complete idea. A comma usually comes before the conjunction in a compound sentence.

Independent clause

A group of words with a subject and a verb. An independent clause expresses a complete thought and can stand alone as a sentence.

EXAMPLE	Subject	Predicate
	Carlo	**took his car to the garage,**

	Conj.	Subject	Predicate
	and	**the mechanic**	**changed the oil.**

A compound sentence tells about two or more related events.

Compound sentence

A sentence made up of two independent clauses joined by a conjunction such as and, but, or or.

EXAMPLE   Correct: The car was old, but it still ran well.

Incorrect: The mechanic changed the oil, and gas costs a lot.

Remember that a simple sentence may have a compound subject or a compound verb. A compound sentence has two or more complete ideas, each with its own subject and verb.

Activity A   Write these compound sentences on your paper. Circle the complete subject in each independent clause. Underline the complete predicate in each independent clause.

1) They were hungry, but all of the restaurants were closed.

2) Alice has a cat, Mike has a gerbil, and Sandy has a hamster.

3) Mr. Barry likes apples, but Mrs. Barry prefers pears and bananas.

4) Lori plays the piano, and her sister plays the flute.

5) Mrs. Castillo gives a lot of homework, but her tests are easy.

Activity B   Number your paper from 1 to 10. Beside each number, write *S* if the sentence is simple. Write *C* if it is compound.

1)   Andrea and Michelle signed up for the play.

2)   He goes fishing every spring but has never caught the big one.

3)   The telephone rang three times, and then it stopped.

4)   The girls hurried, but they were late anyway.

5)   After school, we came right home and did our homework.

6)   The driver stomped hard on the brakes, and the bus skidded.

7)   I met Lydia at the corner, and we walked to school together.

8)   My brother sold his car and bought a van.

9)   Kate and two of her friends signed up for swimming lessons, but the class was full.

10)   The Sunday newspaper has a section designed and written completely by teens.

Activity C   Write five compound sentences. Be sure the ideas are related. Punctuate each sentence correctly.

Part A Number your paper from 1 to 6. Beside each number, write *S* if the sentence is simple. Write *C* if it is compound.

1) Paul plays on the basketball team and works part time at the grocery store.

2) He is an assistant manager in the deli.

3) The store manager hired him as a bagger, but Paul wanted more responsibility.

4) After two months, Mr. Alvarez and Paul talked.

5) Mr. Alvarez offered Paul the job in the deli, and Paul accepted it.

6) It meant more responsibility, but it also meant a raise in pay.

Part B On your paper, write whether the words in bold in these sentences show a *compound subject, compound verb,* or *independent clauses.*

1) Latisha **called me after school** and **asked for help with her project**.

2) **I met her at the library**, and **we went over the assignment**.

3) **Most of the students in the class were writing research papers**, but **she made a different decision**.

4) Latisha **was designing** and **building a model city**.

5) **One of our teachers** and **several of our classmates** were also at the library.

6) Andrea **spotted us** and **came over to our table**.

7) **Andrea, Latisha**, and **I** are in the same math class.

8) **We walked to the bus stop together**, but **Andrea did not get on the bus with Latisha and me**.

9) **Andrea lives close to the library**, so **she walked home**.

10) We **waved good-bye** and **then got on the bus**.

Part A For each item below, write *S* on your paper if the group of words is a sentence. If the group of words is not a sentence, copy it onto your paper and add words to make a complete sentence.

1) The ball landed in the field.

2) As usual, each of the boys on the team.

3) Practicing at four instead of three on Monday.

4) Because of some changes in the team.

5) How does it feel to have a winning record?

Part B Write the following sentences on your paper. Add the correct end marks. Beside each sentence, write its purpose (*Statement, Question, Command or Request, Strong Feeling*).

1) Listen to this

2) She laughed at his joke

3) That was so funny

4) Please tell that joke to LeeAnn

5) Are you really hoping to be a stand-up comic

6) How exciting that would be

7) Many people try but don't make it

8) Experience and talent are the key to success

9) Is there a school for stand-up comics

10) Find out about it

Part C Write each sentence on your paper. Underline the complete subject once and the complete predicate twice. Circle the simple subject and the verb or verb phrase. Remember that the simple subject and the verb can be compound.

1) The car sputtered and came to a stop.
2) What was that strange noise?
3) After a few seconds, the rattling noise stopped, too.
4) His parents and the man at the gas station had warned him about this.
5) Don't buy the car!
6) He did not take their advice and bought the car.
7) Some of his friends did not agree with his decision either.
8) At first, everything was fine.
9) Yesterday, he had driven all the way to Parker City without a problem.
10) Today was a different story.

Part D Write each sentence on your paper. Beside each sentence write whether it is *simple* or *compound*. Then underline the complete subject once and the complete predicate twice in each independent clause.

Example   We drove to the lake on Sunday, and Maria's family came on Monday.—compound

1) Each summer, the two families vacation together.
2) All of them look forward to this vacation, and none of them would miss it.
3) The Dawsons live in the city, but the Ortegas live only a short drive from the lake.
4) Mrs. Ortega and Mrs. Dawson met in college, and they have remained friends since then.
5) Their children have known each other all their lives and get along well.

Test Taking Tip   If you know you will be asked to label parts of a sentence on an English test, write sample sentences. Then practice identifying sentence parts.

Sentence Patterns

I f you do any sewing or woodworking, you know that a pattern often is used as the model for an article you want to make. Languages have patterns, too.

The English language has only a few basic sentence patterns. This chapter focuses on four of those patterns.

Goals for Learning

▶ To identify transitive and intransitive verbs in sentences

▶ To identify the parts of sentences with intransitive verbs

▶ To identify the parts of sentences with direct and indirect objects

▶ To identify the parts of sentences with subject complements

▶ To diagram sentences correctly from each of the four sentence patterns

▶ To diagram sentences with adverbs, adjectives, and prepositional phrases

▶ To diagram compound sentences

Pattern 1 sentences are the simplest kind of sentence pattern. They can express a complete thought with just a subject and verb or verb phrase.

> Pattern 1 Sentence: Subject + Verb

EXAMPLES

S V   S   V
Sue smiled.   The sun was shining.

Activity A   Write each of these Pattern 1 sentences on your paper. Draw a line between the subject and the verb.

Example   The dog / was barking.

1) The ball bounced.

2) My best friend moved.

3) Donna laughed.

4) They were singing.

5) The people on our block are meeting.

Pattern 1 sentences may have adjectives and adverbs. An adjective describes a noun or a pronoun. An adverb tells about the verb. In a Pattern 1 sentence, an adverb may come at the beginning of a sentence or between the helping verb and the main verb.

EXAMPLES

Adj.   Adj.   S   V
The newborn kitten purred.

S   Adv.   V   Adv.
Mr. Edmonds often arrives early.

Adv.   S   V   Adv.
Usually, Nina is late.

Activity B Copy these Pattern 1 sentences onto your paper. Write *S* above the subject, *V* above the verb or verb phrase, *Adj.* above any adjectives, and *Adv.* above any adverbs.

Example   Adj. S   V   Adv.

                The fire was burning brightly.

1) Victor can run fast.

2) That little baby is always smiling.

3) Alison practices often.

4) The old radio works.

5) Yesterday it rained hard.

Activity C Write a Pattern 1 sentence with each of these verbs on your paper. Underline the complete subject once and the complete predicate twice in each sentence.

1) go   **6)** cry

2) ask   **7)** fall

3) work   **8)** scream

4) laugh   **9)** think

5) walk

A Pattern 1 sentence may have a prepositional phrase. The prepositional phrase may be an adjective phrase that describes the subject. It may be an adverb phrase that tells about the verb.

EXAMPLE	
	S Adj. Phrase V
	The boy behind me coughed.
	(Which boy? The one behind me)
	S V Adv. Phrase
	Sue is walking to the store.
	(Where is Sue walking? *to the store*)

Activity D Write each of these Pattern 1 sentences on your paper. Draw a line between the complete subject and complete predicate. Underline the prepositional phrase or phrases in each sentence.

Example Everyone <u>in the audience</u> / laughed <u>at the clown</u>.

1) Jaimie went to school.

2) Mr. DeLeo works at the post office.

3) The gas station on the corner closed.

4) Our friends from Ohio are visiting for two weeks.

5) The pot of flowers fell from the porch.

Activity E Write these Pattern 1 sentences on your paper. Add adjectives and adjective phrases if the subject is bold. Add adverbs and adverb phrases if the verb is bold. Add both if the subject and verb are bold.

Example The girl **walked**.
The girl walked **quickly to the store**.

1) The dog **barked**.

2) **A flower grew**.

3) The boys **left**.

4) **The woman** listened.

5) They **ate**.

6) **Snow fell**.

7) We **talked**.

8) **Roberto** is running.

Activity F Write ten Pattern 1 sentences on your paper.

Remember, a Pattern 1 sentence:

- must have a subject and a verb
- may have an adjective, an adverb, or both
- may have a prepositional phrase

A Pattern 1 sentence may ask a question. Part of the verb may help to form the question and come at the beginning of the sentence.

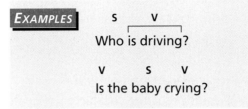

EXAMPLES

S   V
Who is driving?

V   S   V
Is the baby crying?

Activity G   Write these Pattern 1 sentences on your paper. Circle the subject. Underline the verb or verb phrase.

1) Has Mario written?

2) Which book fell off the shelf?

3) Where does Mr. Davis work?

4) Is Annette still practicing?

5) Are you listening to the radio?

6) Did anyone call?

7) Who whistled?

A Pattern 1 sentence may have a compound subject.

EXAMPLE   **Sue** and **Rita** will sing next.

A Pattern 1 sentence may have a compound verb.

EXAMPLE   The band **will march** and **play** in a parade.

Two Pattern 1 sentences may be joined with a conjunction to form a compound sentence.

EXAMPLE   Mrs. Nelson laughed at the joke, **but** Mr. Nelson only smiled.

Activity H   The following Pattern 1 sentences have a compound subject or a compound verb. Some sentences are compound. Write each sentence on your paper. Then follow these directions for each sentence:

- First, underline the complete subject or subjects once.
- Then, circle the simple subjects.
- Next, underline the complete predicate or predicates twice.
- Then, circle the verbs or verb phrases.

1) The book and the pencil fell on the floor.

2) Marilyn was laughing one minute and crying the next.

3) Lisa and Rico were on time, but Alex wasn't.

4) Clarissa studied for her test, and then she went right to sleep.

5) The actors and director came on stage for a final bow, but the writer stayed behind the curtain.

Activity I   Write these Pattern 1 sentences on your paper. Write *S* above the simple subject. Write *V* above the verb or verb phrase.

Example   S   V
                  The Spanish teacher listened closely to her students.

1) The band played loudly at the dance.

2) Mrs. Draper drove off in a hurry.

3) Everyone laughed loudly at the joke.

4) Which student responded to the question?

5) Is your dog barking at my cat again?

6) Several of the people cried during the movie.

7) Emilio's new bike rides smoothly.

8) He asked about the job.

9) Are you leaving for school soon?

10) Our band will travel to Florida and play in front of a large crowd.

Diagramming Pattern 1 Sentences

A sentence diagram is a picture of a sentence that helps us see the parts of the sentence more clearly. When you write a sentence, you put different parts of a sentence together. When you diagram, you separate the parts of the sentence to see how they are put together.

To diagram a Pattern 1 sentence, follow steps 1–3.

1. Find the simple subject and the simple predicate (verb or verb phrase) in the sentence.

> The small **kitten** with the black stripe **purred** softly in my arms.

2. Write the simple subject and the simple predicate on a horizontal line.

3. Draw a short vertical line between the subject and predicate.

EXAMPLE

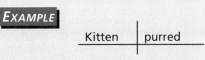

Kitten | purred

Activity J   Diagram these simple Pattern 1 sentences.

Example   Pedro has been working.

Pedro | has been working.

1) Snow fell.

2) Susan is smiling.

3) Music had been playing.

To diagram more complex Pattern 1 sentences, follow these steps.

1. Put the adjectives and prepositional phrases that describe the subject below the subject.

2. Place adjectives on slanted lines.

3. Put the preposition on a slanted line and its object on a horizontal line. Put any words that describe the object of the preposition on slanted lines below it.

4. Put the adverbs and prepositional phrases that describe the verb below the verb.

5. Place adverbs on slanted lines.

EXAMPLE

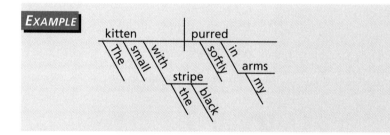

Some Pattern 1 sentences have compound subjects and compound verbs. Some Pattern 1 sentences are compound sentences. These sentences are diagrammed in a special way.

EXAMPLE   Compound subject: **Elise** and **Vanessa** sang.

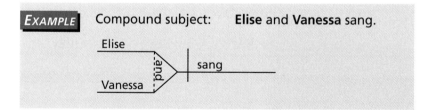

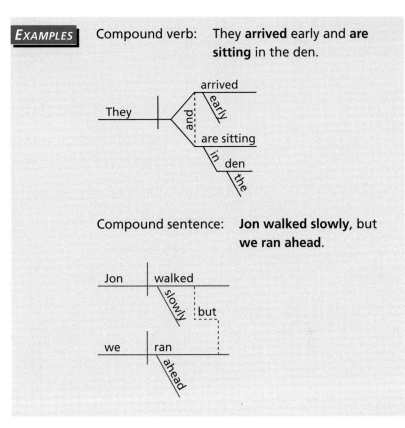

EXAMPLES   Compound verb: They **arrived** early and **are sitting** in the den.

Compound sentence: **Jon walked slowly,** but **we ran ahead.**

Activity K   Diagram these Pattern 1 sentences on your paper. Follow the directions for diagramming that begin on page 227.

1) The school band returned late on Sunday.

2) Everyone on the bus was laughing and singing.

3) Students and parents had been gone for a week.

4) Photographers were everywhere, and reporters wrote quickly.

5) Band members beamed happily into the camera.

6) That group picture was taken after the first event.

Part A Write each of these Pattern 1 sentences on your paper. Underline the complete subject once and the complete predicate twice.

1) Which students are in the band room?

2) Everyone in the band will ride on the bus.

3) My trumpet fell on the floor.

4) Luckily, it did not break.

5) Ramon is waiting for you.

6) Is your book under my desk?

7) Liz and her friend from Dallas are eating at my favorite restaurant.

8) Have you looked for a job recently?

9) They will stay in school and graduate.

10) We have been practicing and preparing for this trip for a long time.

Part B Diagram these Pattern 1 sentences.

1) We were giggling about a silly joke.

2) Mrs. Ozawa spoke softly.

3) The little boy across the street knocked on our door.

4) Tina and Louie work for their father after school.

5) Suddenly, the man arose and left.

6) I listen to all different music, but Sally listens only to rock.

Transitive verb

A verb that shows action passed from the subject of the sentence toward a person or thing.

The two main kinds of verbs are **transitive** and **intransitive**. A transitive verb transfers the action from the subject of a sentence to another person or thing. The person or thing that receives the action is the **direct object**. The direct object is a noun or pronoun.

EXAMPLES   John **threw** the **ball**.
(What did John throw? He threw the ball.)

The coach has **changed pitchers** again.
(What has the coach changed? He has changed pitchers.)

Intransitive verb

A verb that does not transfer action from the subject to an object.

An intransitive verb does not have a direct object. The action is not transferred from the subject to another person or thing. A Pattern 1 sentence has an intransitive verb.

EXAMPLES   She **is laughing**.   The fire **burned**.

Direct object

A noun or pronoun that receives the action from a transitive verb.

A Pattern 2 sentence contains a transitive verb and a direct object. The direct object of the verb is always a noun or pronoun.

Pattern 2 Sentence: Subject + Verb + Direct Object

EXAMPLE

          S   V   D.O.
Mr. Allen made dinner.

Activity A   Write the direct object in each of these sentences on your paper. The verb is in bold.

1) He **found** it.

2) Rosa **took** notes.

3) The teacher **praised** him.

4) The farmer **planted** corn.

Adjectives may be used to describe nouns used as direct objects.

         S   V Adj. Adj. D.O.
Hector sold his old guitar.

Activity B   Write the direct object in each of these sentences on your paper. The verb is in bold. Do not include adjectives.

1) Len **lost** his wallet.
2) They **ate** an early supper.
3) He **is washing** his mom's car.
4) The people next door **are painting** their house.
5) She **sang** a beautiful song.

When a pronoun is the direct object, it is always in the objective form.

Forms of Personal Pronouns		
Singular First person Second person Third person	**Subject** I you he she it	**Object** me you him her it
Plural First person Second person Third person	we you they	us you them

         S   V   D.O.
Marco drove them to school.

Activity C   Write the pronoun on your paper that should appear in each sentence to make it correct. Remember that a pronoun used as a direct object is always in the objective form.

1) Did you see (he, him)?
2) Fred saw (she, her) at the library.
3) Before he put on his sneakers, he cleaned (they, them).
4) Tina helped (we, us) with our math homework.
5) He likes (I, me).

Activity D   Create three columns on your paper with the headings *Subject, Verb,* and *Direct Object.* Then identify the simple subject, the verb, and the direct object in each sentence and write them in the correct column.

Example   My Aunt Anita rented a small apartment.

Subject	Verb	Direct Object
Aunt Anita	rented	apartment

1) The cat chased the mouse.

2) I have been studying a new language.

3) The brave firefighters climbed the ladders.

4) Mr. Cha loves that old song!

5) We did not see her.

The complete predicate of a Pattern 2 sentence must have a verb and an object. It may also have an adverb.

EXAMPLES

    Adv.   S   V   D.O.
Luckily, Sandy found her notebook.

    S   V   D.O.   Adv.
Matt saw a great movie yesterday.

S Adv.   V   D.O.
I just found it.

Activity E   Write the complete predicate in each of these sentences on your paper. (HINT: Find the complete subject first. All of the words left over are in the predicate.)

1) Leon bought his tickets early.

2) You can make dinner now.

3) Kevin ate his dinner quickly.

4) She just woke up.

5) Yesterday Dan lost his favorite baseball cap.

The predicate part of a Pattern 2 sentence may have a prepositional phrase that tells about the verb, the direct object, or both.

> **EXAMPLES**
>
> ```
>              S    V    D.O.  Prep. Phrase
> ```
> Sabrina ate tacos for dinner.
> (*For dinner* is an adverb phrase that tells about the verb *ate*. When did Sabrina eat tacos? *for dinner.*)
>
> ```
>          S      V        D.O.    Prep. Phrase
> ```
> Sabrina ate both tacos on her dish.
> (*On her dish* is an adjective phrase that describes *tacos*. Which tacos? the ones *on her dish.*)
>
> ```
>   Adv. Phrase     S    V     D.O.     Adj. Phrase
> ```
> After dinner, we played a game of Monopoly.
> (When did they play? *after dinner.* What kind of game? *of Monopoly.*)

Activity F   Write the complete predicate in each of these sentences on your paper. Then underline the verb once and the direct object twice. Circle each prepositional phrase. Draw an arrow from the prepositional phrase to the word it tells about.

Example   Tómas painted the house on the corner on Friday.

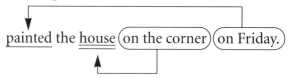

1) Carol wrote a letter to her uncle Albert.
2) Sara bought the blue sneakers with the white trim.
3) He carried the two bags of groceries into the house.
4) Before school, we fed the fish in the tank.

Activity G   Write Pattern 2 sentences for each verb below on your paper. Each sentence must have a subject, a verb, and an object. You may also add adjectives, adverbs, and prepositional phrases.

1) break   4) dig   7) catch
2) make   5) freeze   8) spend
3) bought   6) chase   9) played

Pattern 2 sentences may be questions. In some questions that begin with the interrogative pronouns *who, which,* and *what,* the direct object of the verb begins the sentence. Remember, also, that in questions, part of the verb may come before the subject to help form the question.

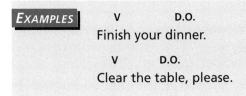

EXAMPLES

D.O. V S V
What did you see? (You did see what.)

V S V D.O.
Did I see a deer at the window? (I did see a deer.)

Activity H Find the verb or verb phrase and the direct object in each sentence. Write them on your paper. If you are not sure which word is the direct object, try turning the question into a statement.

1) Have you read that article?
2) Whom did she ask to the dance?
3) May I have a piece of pizza?
4) What will he do after graduation?
5) Which of these do you want?

Pattern 2 sentences may also be commands or requests. Remember that the subject of a command or request is always understood to be *you.* The word *you* may or may not appear.

EXAMPLES

V D.O.
Finish your dinner.

V D.O.
Clear the table, please.

Activity I Write each of these sentences on your paper. Circle the verb. Underline the direct object.

1) Take this book to the library.
2) Make vegetable soup for supper, please.
3) Complete your essay at home.
4) Hang your coat in the closet.
5) Have some more soup.

A Pattern 2 sentence may have a compound verb and a compound object. You may join two Pattern 2 sentences together with a conjunction to make a compound sentence.

> **EXAMPLES**
>
> Compound verb: We **cooked** and **served** dinner.
>
> Compound direct object: She will play **basketball** or **soccer**.
>
> Compound sentence: **I** saw Paul, but **he didn't have my book.**

Each part of the compound verb may have its own direct object.

> **EXAMPLE**
>
> S V   D.O.   V D.O
> We made the pizza and put it in the oven.

Activity J Read each of these Pattern 2 sentences. Write on your paper whether the sentence has a compound verb, has a compound object, or is a compound sentence. Then write the compound verb, compound object, or two independent clauses.

Example We made supper and then cleaned the kitchen.
compound verb—made, cleaned

1) Are you reading that book or this one?

2) We enjoyed the party but left early.

3) They returned the wallet and its contents to the owner.

4) LeeAn bought the dress on Monday, but she returned it on Tuesday.

5) She saves most of her pay for college and uses the rest for spending money.

6) Virginia plays the piano and the violin.

7) Complete the test and bring it to me.

8) Tim has a part-time job; however, he also takes classes at the community college.

Diagramming Pattern 2 Sentences

To diagram a Pattern 2 sentence:

1. Identify the subject, verb, and direct object.

2. Place the object on the baseline with the subject and verb.

3. Draw a short vertical line to separate the verb and the direct object.

> **EXAMPLE** We carefully slid the two loaves of bread into the oven.

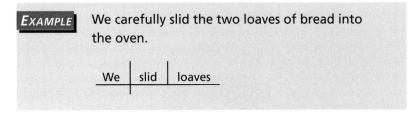

4. Put each adverb, adjective, or prepositional phrase under the word it is describing or telling about.

> **EXAMPLE**

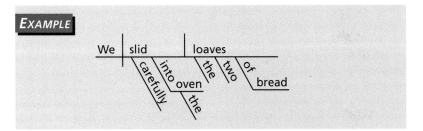

5. Show the understood subject of a command or a request in parentheses.

> **EXAMPLE** Change that flat tire quickly.

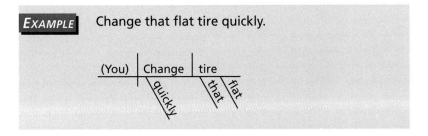

6. If the sentence is a question, change it into a statement. Then draw the diagram.

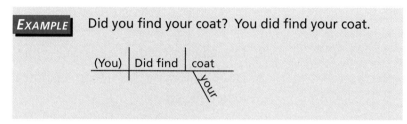

EXAMPLE Did you find your coat? You did find your coat.

7. Diagram Pattern 2 sentences that have compound verbs or compound objects like this.

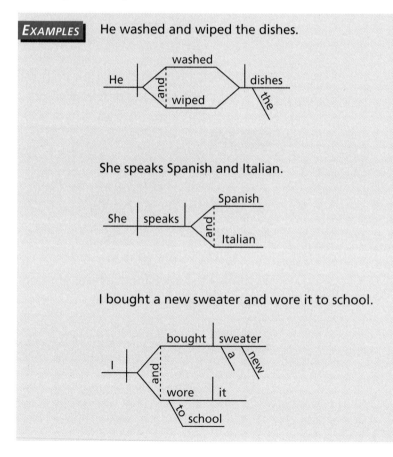

EXAMPLES He washed and wiped the dishes.

She speaks Spanish and Italian.

I bought a new sweater and wore it to school.

Compound Pattern 2 sentences contain two independent clauses that each express a complete thought.

To diagram a compound sentence:

1. Place each independent clause on its own baseline.

2. Join the two clauses with a dotted line.

 Elena wrote the story, and Jeff drew the pictures.

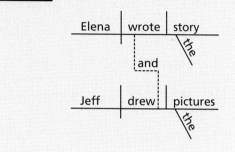

Activity K Diagram these sentences. Look at the examples on pages 237–238.

1) Stop that noise immediately!

2) Jack left his notebook and pen in his locker.

3) Have you seen Sally?

4) Tia likes poetry by Edgar Allan Poe.

5) Mr. Caruso has blue eyes, and his wife has brown eyes.

6) We bought our tickets for the late show and then had dinner.

7) He fixed the car, but it still had a problem.

8) Do you want the soup or the salad with your meal?

9) They scraped and painted the house.

Part A Write the direct object in each of these sentences on your paper. Some sentences may have more than one direct object.

1) Evan's dad sells computers.

2) The teacher answered the questions.

3) Laura described her new dress to her friends.

4) The museum guard checked our tickets.

5) Loni ordered shrimp and broccoli for lunch.

Part B Diagram these Pattern 2 sentences.

1) Have you seen that movie?

2) He dropped his pen and book onto the floor.

3) Inez made an outline and then wrote her report.

4) What will you do during vacation?

5) First, read the book, and then see the movie.

6) He read an interesting article about UFOs recently.

7) Knead the dough well and shape it into loaves.

8) Otis recited the long poem without a single mistake.

Indirect object

A noun or pronoun that comes after the verb and before the direct object and usually answers the question to whom, to what, from whom, *or* for what *about the verb.*

A Pattern 3 sentence has a transitive verb, a direct object, and an **indirect object**. The indirect object tells who will receive the direct object. An indirect object is a noun or pronoun that names the person receiving the direct object.

The indirect object comes after the verb and before the direct object in a sentence.

An indirect object answers the question *to whom, to what, for whom,* or *for what* about the verb.

> Pattern 3 Sentence:
> Subject + Verb + Indirect Object + Direct Object

 EXAMPLE

    S   V   Ind. O. D.O.
Karyn wrote Mark a letter.
(Karyn wrote a letter *to whom?* She wrote to Mark.)

Activity A　Write the indirect objects in each of these sentences on your paper. (HINT: To find the indirect object, ask the question *to whom, to what, for whom,* or *for what* about the verb.)

1) Joanna gave her mother a gift.

2) I wrote myself a reminder.

3) The school mailed students their final report cards.

4) I offered Chan some pizza.

5) Mrs. López brought me my homework.

6) Marlene showed me her baseball card collection.

7) The bank lent Mr. Nakai money.

8) The salesclerk handed Maya the change.

9) Joseph sold Jon his old bike.

10) The woman bought her twin daughters matching outfits.

An indirect object is never part of a prepositional phrase.

Indirect object: He wrote **me** a letter.

Object of a preposition: He wrote a letter to **me**.

Activity B   Decide whether the word in bold is an indirect object or the object of a preposition. Write *indirect object* or *object of a preposition* on your paper.

1) Lou gave his **dog** a bone.

2) Helena poured some milk for her **cat**.

3) The store sent coupons to their best **customers**.

4) The server brought **us** lunch.

5) Mrs. Jenkins handed my paycheck to **me**.

Activity C   Create four columns on your paper with the headings *Subject, Verb, Indirect Object,* and *Direct Object*. Then identify the simple subject, the verb, the indirect object, and the direct object in each sentence. Write these in the correct column.

Example   Mary gave me a birthday present.

Subject	Verb	Indirect Object	Direct Object
Mary	gave	me	present

1) The director gave the band members their music.

2) Fred asked Mr. Smith a question.

3) The music company sent the school a bill.

4) The secretary handed his boss the mail.

5) Mrs. Arloff offered the students her help.

6) The teacher gave the class homework.

7) She taught her friend sign language.

8) Jenny wrote her aunt a letter.

9) The school awarded Tim a scholarship.

10) Mr. Jackson gave every employee a raise.

When the indirect object is a pronoun, the pronoun must be in the objective case. Refer to the chart on page 232.

> **EXAMPLE**
>
> | S | V | Ind. O. | D.O. |
> |---|---|---------|------|
> His boss offered him a promotion.

Activity D   Write the pronoun on your paper that should appear in each sentence to make it correct. Remember that a pronoun used as an indirect object is always in the objective form.

1) Tom gave (I, me) the message.

2) Fred sent (he, him) a letter.

3) Martha told (she, her) the answer.

4) That teacher taught (we, us) Spanish.

5) We served (they, them) dinner.

Pattern 3 sentences may have adjectives and prepositional phrases that describe the indirect object.

> **EXAMPLES**
>
> | S | V | Adj. | Adj | Ind.O. | D.O. |
> |---|---|------|-----|--------|------|
> Steve wrote his younger sister a letter.
>
> | S | V | Adj. | Ind. O. | Prep. Phrase | D.O. |
> |---|---|------|---------|--------------|------|
> She gave her friend from Montana a gift.

Activity E   Rewrite each of these sentences on your paper. Add an adjective or prepositional phrase to describe the indirect object in bold.

1) Pat sent her **friend** a message.

2) Marcus offered the **woman** his seat.

3) The teacher told the **boy** the answer.

4) We made our **neighbor** an offer.

5) We asked the **mechanic** a question about the car.

Pattern 3 sentences may be questions. Part of the verb phrase may come before the subject. The question may begin with an interrogative word.

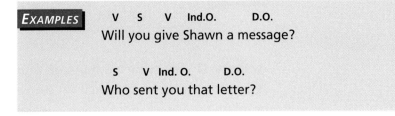

EXAMPLES

| | V | S | V | Ind.O. | D.O. |

V   S   V   Ind.O.   D.O.
Will you give Shawn a message?

S   V Ind. O.   D.O.
Who sent you that letter?

Pattern 3 sentences are often commands or requests.

EXAMPLES

S   V   Ind.O.   D.O.
(You) Show the class your drawing.

S   V Ind.O.   D.O.
(You) Give me his new address.

Activity F   Write the indirect objects in these sentences on your paper.

1) Tell me the answer.

2) Did you give the dog a biscuit?

3) Would you lend me your sweater for the evening?

4) Please teach me Spanish.

5) When did Anna write you that note?

6) Allow yourself enough time for breakfast.

7) Are you giving Michael a present?

8) Who asked me that question?

9) Bring them their coats.

10) Tell us the truth.

The indirect object of a Pattern 3 sentence can be compound.

Fix your **father** and his **friend** some lunch.

Will you give **Tim** and **Simon** a message?

Maria read her younger **brother** and **sister** a bedtime story.

Activity G   Complete each of these sentences with a compound indirect object. Write the completed sentences on your paper.

1) Write _____ a letter.

2) Give _____ more time.

3) Please tell _____ the answer.

4) Uncle Fred made _____ model airplanes.

5) Would you lend _____ five dollars?

6) I offered _____ more pizza.

7) Joe asked _____ for help with his project.

8) Kim sent _____ birthday gifts.

Activity H   Rearrange each group of words to make a Pattern 3 sentence. Write the sentences on your paper.

1) them served we dinner the

2) gave rose Erica Julio a

3) told team the coach play the the

4) myself snack fixed I a

5) a him he handed dollar

Diagramming Pattern 3 Sentences

To diagram a Pattern 3 sentence:

1. Draw a slanted line and a horizontal line under the verb.

2. Leave the slanted line blank.

3. Write the indirect object on the horizontal line.

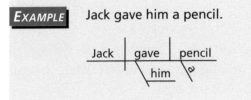

> **EXAMPLE** Jack gave him a pencil.
>
> Jack | gave | pencil
> him a

4. Diagram a compound indirect object this way.

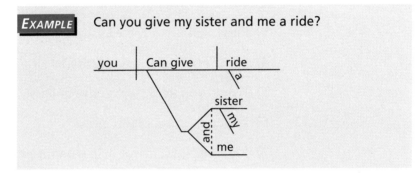

> **EXAMPLE** Can you give my sister and me a ride?
>
> you | Can give | ride
> a
> sister
> my
> and
> me

Activity I   Diagram these Pattern 3 sentences on your paper. Look at the examples above and on pages 237–238.

1) Pass me the bread.

2) Jack lent Larry his car.

3) Jane made Yolanda an offer for her bike.

4) Lana sent her aunt and her uncles thank-you notes.

5) Will you bring Tina and me an apple?

Part A Write the indirect objects in these sentences on your paper.

1) Sue brought Rita and Pam some books.

2) After dinner, Grandpa told the family some old stories.

3) Tim asked his grandfather a question.

4) Will you tell me the story about Dad again?

5) Allow yourself several hours for that report.

6) The members of the team gave Kerry an award for her outstanding effort.

7) Give me another chance at the game, please.

8) Chris handed Tómas and Leon their books.

9) Who sold you that bike?

10) Will you make Sam and me some lunch?

Part B Diagram these Pattern 3 sentences on your paper.

1) My uncle offered me a job in his store.

2) She wrote him a long letter.

3) Dan gave Meg and Lian a ride to work.

4) Who gave you that book?

5) Sing me your song, and then I will give you my opinion.

6) Corey brought her mom and dad breakfast in bed.

7) I sent each guest an invitation and directions to my house.

Complement

The part of a sentence that completes the meaning of the verb.

A Pattern 4 sentence has a transitive verb, a direct object, and an objective complement. A **complement** is a word that completes an idea. An **objective complement** is a noun or an adjective that adds to the meaning of the direct object. The objective complement comes after the direct object in the sentence.

Objective complement

A noun or an adjective that follows a direct object and adds to its meaning.

> Pattern 4 Sentence:
> Subject + Verb + Direct Object + Objective Complement

EXAMPLES

          S   V   D.O. Complement
The Smiths named their baby Christopher.

(*Christopher* is a noun that renames the direct object *baby*.)

          S   V   D.O. Complement
Our neighbors painted their house blue.

(*Blue* is an adjective that adds to the meaning of the direct object *house*.)

Activity A Write the objective complements in these sentences on your paper.

1) The people elected George Washington president in 1788.

2) The frost turned the leaves many colors.

3) Happiness made the girl beautiful.

4) The police found the man dazed.

5) The dark room made us sleepy.

6) Everyone calls Anthony Hopkins a great actor.

7) They made Mrs. Schwartz president of the company.

8) Emilio considers Alison smart.

9) Are you making the tacos spicy?

10) The hot sun turned the grass brown.

Activity B   Write these sentences on your paper. Add a noun or an adjective used as an objective complement. Be sure your sentences make sense.

1) He found science class _____.

2) The artist made the pictures _____.

3) We elected Danny _____.

4) Don't make the soup _____.

5) They called him _____.

6) Teenagers often consider adults _____.

7) Most of the students in Mr. Alvarez's math class find his tests _____.

8) The hot oven turned the pizza dough _____.

Activity C   Write Pattern 4 sentences on your paper using the verbs below.

1) make or made

2) elect or elected

3) find or found

4) name or named

5) turn or turned

6) call or called

7) consider or considered

8) paint or painted

9) judge or judged

10) declare or declared

Diagramming Pattern 4 Sentences

To diagram a Pattern 4 sentence:

1. Place the objective complement on the baseline of the diagram next to the direct object.

2. Separate the objective complement from the direct object with a line slanted toward the direct object.

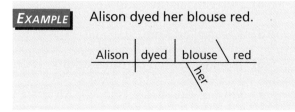

EXAMPLE   Alison dyed her blouse red.

Activity D   Diagram the following Pattern 4 sentences on your paper.

1) Jerry found his computer class interesting.

2) The students elected Jack treasurer.

3) She made the chili spicy.

4) They named Mrs. Santiago "Woman of the Year."

5) Grace painted her room yellow.

6) They called the cottage "Our Escape."

7) We declare Jodie winner.

8) The cold water turned her lips blue.

9) They judged his act excellent.

10) Who considers her latest book dull?

Part A Write the objective complements in these sentences on your paper.

1) They declared the young boy the winner.

2) We made Joe group leader.

3) They call their hamster Swifty.

4) Old age has turned the dog's hair silver.

5) They dyed the wool many colors.

6) You made that meal delicious!

7) We named the little white kitten Snowball.

8) Did you find that program interesting?

9) What makes him so shy?

10) Do you consider yourself an expert on the subject?

Part B Diagram these Pattern 4 sentences on your paper.

1) The wind turned the day cold.

2) The class will elect Carlotta president.

3) Can we call the puppy Pooch?

4) May and Danzel found the play boring.

5) She painted the inside of her closet purple.

Part A   Decide whether the verb in bold in these sentences is transitive or intransitive. Write *transitive* or *intransitive* on your paper.

1) One day Mr. Ellis **bought** a computer.

2) He **called** it an investment in their future.

3) The younger children **clapped** with glee.

4) He **plugged** a modem into the computer.

5) The puppy just **stared** at the computer screen.

6) **Can** we **use** it?

7) They **could play** video games.

8) Mrs. Ellis **keeps** a daily journal on the computer.

9) They **used** it for their tax records.

10) That computer **ran** all evening!

Part B   Write the words in bold in these sentences on your paper. Beside each word, write whether it is the *subject, verb* or *verb phrase, direct object, indirect object, object of the preposition,* or *objective complement.*

1) We gave **Jiro** a CD for his **birthday**.

2) The **Rolling Stones recorded** that song.

3) **Some** of us are going to the movies.

4) **Have** you **read** that book?

5) **Hand me** that hammer, please.

6) The **band** raised **money** for the trip.

7) We elected **John president**.

8) Where are **you** and **Jackie** sitting?

9) **Which** of **these** do you want?

10) Will **you** give **us** a ride?

Part C Write two sentences on your paper for each of the four patterns. Follow the examples.

Pattern 1:	Subject + Verb
	The frightened girl screamed.
Pattern 2:	Subject + Verb + Direct Object
	Mary read her report to the class.
Pattern 3:	Subject + Verb + Indirect and Direct Objects
	Paco gave the puppy a bath.
Pattern 4:	Subject + Verb + Direct Object + Objective Complement
	Connie considers raw vegetables a healthy snack.

Part D Diagram the following sentences.

1) Which of these do you want?

2) Kevin writes music and lyrics.

3) Kevin's music has variety, and his lyrics have real meaning.

4) He named it "Melody" and sang it for Julia.

5) We can make our own birthday cards on the computer.

6) He has been at the computer for hours.

7) They named their computer "The Whiz."

8) Try it yourself.

9) I can add fast, but the computer adds faster.

10) Walter and Andrea asked their mom a question about the computer.

Test Taking Tip Before you answer any questions on a test, skim through the whole test to find out what is expected of you.

Sentence Patterns With a Linking Verb

12

Some artists place pieces of glass or stone in a pattern to make a picture. These patterned pictures are called mosaics. In Chapter 11, you learned that sentences have patterns, too. In this chapter, you will learn about sentence patterns that contain linking verbs.

A linking verb, or state-of-being verb, does not express action. Since a linking verb is intransitive, it does not take a direct object.

Each lesson in Chapter 12 focuses on sentences with linking verbs and shows how to diagram these sentences.

Goals for Learning

▶ To identify the parts of sentences with linking verbs

▶ To distinguish between predicate adjectives and predicate nouns

▶ To diagram sentences with linking verbs

▶ To diagram sentences with adverbs of degree correctly

▶ To diagram compound sentences with linking verbs correctly

Before you learn about Pattern 5 sentences, you need to understand more about verbs.

Linking Verbs

Linking verb

A verb that joins the subject to a noun, pronoun, or adjective in the predicate; it is also called a state-of-being verb.

An action verb expresses action in a sentence. A **linking verb**, or state-of-being verb, does not express action.

EXAMPLES   Action verb: James **plays** baseball.

Linking verb: James **is** a baseball player.

A linking verb joins the subject to a word in the predicate part of the sentence. That word can be a noun, a pronoun, or an adjective. It helps the sentence express a complete thought.

EXAMPLES   Incomplete sentence: This book is.

Complete sentence: This book is new.

A linking verb is intransitive. It never takes a direct object. Sentences with linking verbs follow two patterns:

Subject—Linking Verb—Adjective

Subject—Linking Verb—Noun or Pronoun

EXAMPLES   S   L.V. Adj.
Paul is tall.

S   L.V.   N
Paul is a student.

Predicate adjective

An adjective used after a linking verb. It completes the predicate but describes the subject of the sentence.

An adjective always describes a noun or pronoun. When an adjective appears after a linking verb, the adjective describes the subject. This adjective is called a **predicate adjective**. It is part of the complete predicate, but it describes the subject of the sentence.

> **EXAMPLE**
>
> | Subject | Complete Predicate |
> | --- | --- |
>
> The weather / is **sunny** and **mild** today.
> (*Sunny* and *mild* are adjectives. What *is sunny and mild*? the *weather is*.)

Activity A   Write these sentences on your paper. Circle the linking verb. Underline the predicate adjective or adjectives.

Example   My brother (is) <u>funny</u>.

1) New cars can be expensive.
2) That little boy looks tired.
3) My youngest brother grows taller and taller.
4) He was never shy.
5) Tomorrow will be warm and sunny.
6) Cara and Lee Ann were excited.
7) The baby looked hungry and cranky.
8) Joaquim is never angry.

Pattern 5 Sentences

A Pattern 5 sentence has a subject, a linking verb, and a predicate adjective. The predicate adjective describes the subject.

> Pattern 5 Sentences: Subject + Linking Verb + Adjective

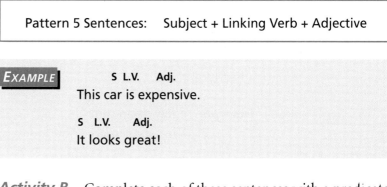

> **EXAMPLE**
>
> S L.V.   Adj.
> This car is expensive.
>
> S L.V.   Adj.
> It looks great!

Activity B   Complete each of these sentences with a predicate adjective. Write the completed sentence on your paper.

1) Today the air feels _____.
2) The sky looks _____.
3) The day has been _____.
4) Everyone seems _____.
5) They appear _____.

Activity C   Create three columns on your paper with the titles *Subject, Linking Verb,* and *Predicate Adjective.* Then identify the simple subject, the linking verb, and the predicate adjective in each sentence. Write them in the correct column.

Example   Jim's report was interesting.

Subject	Linking Verb	Predicate Adjective
report	was	interesting

1) My cousin is artistic.
2) The sauce tasted spicy.
3) That note sounds flat.
4) The little girl became sleepy.
5) The weather turned cold.
6) The young actor appeared nervous.

A Pattern 5 sentence may have an adverb of degree to tell about the predicate adjective. Adverbs of degree answer questions about adjectives.

EXAMPLE

```
            S    L.V.    Adv. Pred. Adj.
Her voice sounded very loud.
```

Activity D   Write these sentences on your paper. Add an adverb of degree to each sentence to tell about the predicate adjective in bold.

Example   I feel **good** today.
            I feel **extremely** good today.

1) My grandparents keep **active**.
2) She looks **happy**.
3) He sounds **tired**.
4) The day turned **cold**.
5) They appeared **calm**.
6) You seem **worried**.
7) The children became **restless**.

A Pattern 5 sentence may have adverbs and prepositional phrases that give more information about the predicate adjective.

> **EXAMPLE** She is always busy after school.
>
> How often? *always*
>
> When? *after school*

Activity E Write these sentences on your paper. Underline the predicate adjectives in each sentence. Then add adverbs or prepositional phrases that tell about each predicate adjective.

1) Jim is tall.

2) That house looks run-down.

3) The sky grew dark.

4) Your painting is colorful.

5) This salad tastes delicious.

6) Your motor sounds odd.

7) Lydia seems quiet.

8) Her notebook is neat.

Activity F Copy these sentences onto your paper. Write *S* above the simple subject, *L.V.* above the linking verb, and *Pred. Adj.* above the predicate adjective.

                S   L.V.   Pred. Adj.

Example The old house looked empty.

1) The month of June is usually pleasant.

2) The days grow longer then.

3) The air feels warmer in June.

4) Maryanne is especially happy about warm weather.

5) The cat becomes friskier, too.

In a Pattern 5 sentence, the predicate adjective may be compound.

> **EXAMPLE**
>
>   S   L.V.   Adj.   Adj.
> Nina's report was **short** and **funny**.

Activity G Complete each of these sentences with compound predicate adjectives. Write the completed sentences on your paper.

1) The new curtains were _____ and _____.

2) Maryanne's speech will be _____ or _____.

3) Andy's new bike is _____ but not _____.

4) The month of May is _____ and _____.

5) After a big dinner, I am usually _____ and _____.

You may combine two Pattern 5 sentences with a conjunction to form a compound sentence. A compound sentence has two complete thoughts.

> **EXAMPLE**
>
>   S   L.V.   Adj.   S   L.V.   Adj.
> Mrs. Davis is usually serious, but Mr. Davis is always funny.

Activity H First, write two related Pattern 5 sentences. Then use one of the following conjunctions to combine the two sentences into a compound sentence.

               and   for   or   but

A Pattern 5 sentence may be a command or request. Remember that commands are always in the present tense. Use the infinitive form of linking verbs in commands.

> **EXAMPLE**
>
> L.V. Pred. Adj.
> Be quiet.

Activity I   Copy these commands or requests onto your paper. Underline the linking verb once and the predicate adjective or compound predicate adjective twice.

Example   Keep <u>quiet</u> during my report!

1) Look friendly during the job interview.

2) Be nice to your teacher!

3) Stay calm during an emergency.

4) Be ready for your class.

5) Remain loyal and true to your friends.

A Pattern 5 sentence may also be a question. In a Pattern 5 question, the predicate adjective may come right after the subject. The verb or part of a verb phrase may be used to form the question.

| EXAMPLES | L.V. | S | L.V. | Pred. Adj. |

Did his report seem short?

L.V.   S   Compound Pred. Adj.

Was April warm and rainy?

Activity J   Copy these sentences onto your paper. Circle the subject. Underline the linking verb once and the predicate adjective or compound predicate adjective twice.

Example   <u>Is</u> your (brother) <u>upset</u> about something?

1) Are you tired and hungry?

2) Does the school day seem longer to you?

3) Is this bread homemade?

4) Was she excited or nervous about the play?

5) Will these flowers stay fresh until Friday?

Diagramming Pattern 5 Sentences

To diagram a Pattern 5 sentence:

1. Place the predicate adjective on the baseline of the diagram.

2. Separate the predicate adjective from the verb with a short line slanted toward the verb.

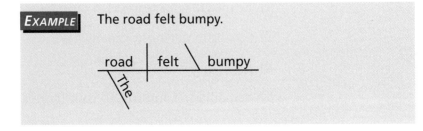

EXAMPLE   The road felt bumpy.

3. Diagram a compound predicate adjective this way.

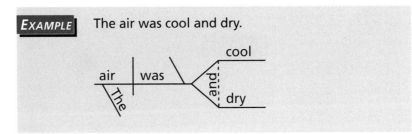

EXAMPLE   The air was cool and dry.

4. Place an adverb of degree under the adjective on a slanted line.

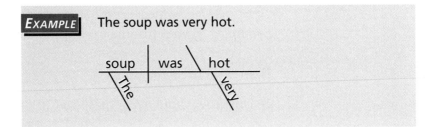

EXAMPLE   The soup was very hot.

5. Show the understood subject of a command or a request in parentheses.

Be kind.

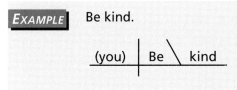

6. If a Pattern 5 sentence is a question, change it into a statement. Then draw the diagram.

Was your trip fun? Your trip was fun.

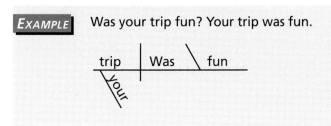

To diagram a compound Pattern 5 sentence:

1. Place each complete thought on its own baseline.
2. Connect each thought with a dotted line.

Mrs. Davis is usually serious, but Mr. Davis is always funny.

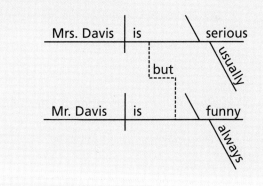

Activity K   Diagram these Pattern 5 sentences on your paper. If you need help, look at the rules and examples on page 262 and above.

1) Monday morning was extremely windy, but the air was warm.
2) Stay quiet and absolutely still.
3) Is your puppy afraid of loud noises?

Part A Write whether the verb in bold in each sentence is a *linking verb* or an *action verb*. Write your answers on your paper. Remember, a linking verb never takes a direct object.

1) **Be** loyal to your friends.

2) Later I **am going** to the movies.

3) **Taste** this stew for me.

4) **Is** it too salty?

5) No, it **tastes** just right!

Part B Write the linking verbs and predicate adjectives in each of these sentences on your paper.

1) The lemon tasted sour.

2) Sue appears friendly.

3) James is very athletic.

4) Have they always been so active?

5) That computer is small but powerful.

Part C Diagram these Pattern 5 sentences on your paper.

1) Today the air feels chilly.

2) Everyone seemed happy and carefree.

3) Be careful on that ladder!

4) Was my speech too long?

Predicate nominative

A noun or pronoun that follows a linking verb and renames the subject.

A Pattern 6 sentence has a subject, a linking verb, and a **predicate nominative**. The predicate nominative is a noun or pronoun that renames the subject. Like a predicate adjective, a predicate nominative always follows a linking verb.

Pattern 6 Sentences: Subject + Linking Verb + Noun or Pronoun
---

               S   L.V.   P.N.
           That building was once a school.

Activity A Write these sentences on your paper. Write *S* above the subject, *L.V.* above the linking verb, and *P.N.* above the predicate nominative.

                S   L.V.   P.N.
Example Miss Lewis has been our coach.

1) In 1789, George Washington became president.

2) She is my friend.

3) My favorite horror movie is *The Invasion of the Body Snatchers.*

4) The song writer is also a poet.

5) The winner of the race was Emily.

6) They are athletes.

7) The woman in the picture is a neighbor.

8) Charles will be the director.

9) My choice for class president is you.

10) The title of that play is *Raisin in the Sun.*

In a Pattern 6 sentence, adjectives often come before the predicate nominative. The adjective describes the predicate nominative.

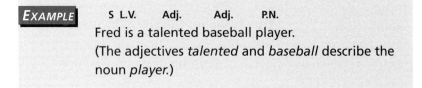

| | S | L.V. | Adj. | Adj. | P.N. |
EXAMPLE

S   L.V.   Adj.   Adj.   P.N.
Fred is a talented baseball player.
(The adjectives *talented* and *baseball* describe the noun *player*.)

Activity B   Write these sentences on your paper. Circle the predicate nominative and underline the adjectives that describe it in each sentence. Do not include the articles *the, a,* or *an.*

1) George Washington was the first president.

2) Aunt Marie is a great cook.

3) Carol has always been a friendly, helpful person.

4) Ted has become an excellent soccer coach.

5) Mrs. Marino is a popular teacher.

Do not confuse a noun or pronoun used as a direct object with a predicate nominative. Remember, a direct object receives the action of a transitive verb. A predicate nominative follows an intransitive verb and renames the subject.

EXAMPLE

Direct object: Ramona introduced the **musician**.
                 (*Musician* receives the action of the transitive verb *introduced*.)

Predicate
nominative: Ramona is a **musician**. (*Musician* renames the subject *Ramona*.)

Activity C   Write on your paper whether the word in bold is a *direct object* or a *predicate nominative.*

1) James plays **baseball** in the spring.

2) He is the team **captain**.

3) Tony is the league's best **catcher**.

4) He can also hit the **ball** a mile.

5) He is one of the team's best **hitters**.

A Pattern 6 sentence may have an adverb or a prepositional phrase that answers questions about the linking verb.

 EXAMPLES   Larry is **always** a good friend.
(When is Larry a good friend? *always*)

He has been my friend **for years**.
(How long has he been a friend? *for years*)

A Pattern 6 sentence may have a prepositional phrase that describes the predicate nominative.

 EXAMPLE   Agatha Christie was the author **of many books**.
(What kind of author? An author *of many books*)

Activity D   Write the predicate nominatives in these sentences on your paper. Remember, the predicate nominative is never the object of a preposition.

1) Uruguay is a country in South America.

2) The Nile is one of the world's longest rivers.

3) Mars is the closest planet to the Earth.

4) Pasta has been a popular food in the United States.

5) The most popular movie of 1939 was probably *Gone With the Wind*.

6) *Star Wars* is still Andy's favorite movie.

7) Dana has been Anne's best friend for two years.

Activity E   Write five Pattern 6 sentences on your paper. Add as many adverbs, adjectives, and prepositional phrases as you wish. For each sentence, write *S* above the subject, *L.V.* above the linking verb, and *P.N.* above the predicate nominative.

             S   L.V.   P.N.

Example   Alicia has been Cyndi's best friend since first grade.

A Pattern 6 sentence may be a command or a request.

> **EXAMPLES**
>
>   L.V.   P.N.
> Be an honest person.
>
>   L.V.   P.N.
> Always remain a loyal friend.

A Pattern 6 sentence may also be a question.

> **EXAMPLES**
>
>   L.V. S   L.V. P.N.
> Have they always been friends?
>
>   L.V. S   P.N.
> Were you the winner?

A Pattern 6 sentence may have compound parts.

> **EXAMPLE**
>
>   S   S L.V.   P.N.   P.N.
> Marissa and Sandra are excellent students and super athletes.

You may combine two Pattern 6 sentences with a conjunction to form a compound sentence.

> **EXAMPLE**
>
>   S L.V.   P.N.   S L.V. P.N.
> Annie is class president now, and last year she was treasurer.

Activity F   Write these sentences on your paper. Write *S* above the subject, *L.V.* above the linking verb, and *P.N.* above the predicate nominative. If a subject is understood, write it in. Some sentences may have compound parts or may be compound sentences.

1) Was Franklin Pierce a U.S. president?

2) Are those oak trees or maple trees?

3) Become a success for your own satisfaction.

4) *The Good Earth* is a movie and a book.

5) Phil is a student now, but he will be an architect some day.

Diagramming Pattern 6 Sentences

To diagram a Pattern 6 sentence:

1. Place the predicate nominative on the baseline of the diagram.

2. Separate the predicate nominative from the verb with a line slanted toward the verb.

EXAMPLE   Mrs. Castillo is a Spanish teacher.

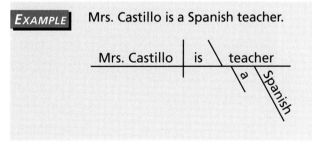

3. Diagram a compound predicate nominative this way.

EXAMPLE   Teri is a student and an athlete.

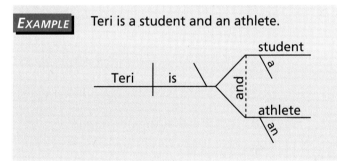

4. If a Pattern 6 sentence is a question, change the question to a statement. Then diagram it.

EXAMPLE   **Question**   **Statement**
Is that an oak tree? → That is an oak tree.

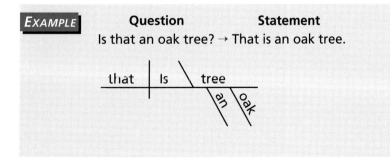

5. Put the understood subject of a command in parentheses.

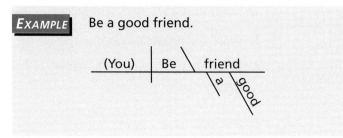

EXAMPLE   Be a good friend.

Activity G   Diagram these Pattern 6 sentences on your paper.

1) Who is she?

2) Kim became our class secretary.

3) Sue and Kelly have become good friends.

4) Two popular sports are football and baseball.

5) Paul Dunbar was a poet, and he was a novelist.

6) These are some of my favorite drawings.

7) Remain a person of good character.

8) What is that in your hand?

9) Annie has always been a great speaker, but she has never been a good listener.

10) Were you the one in the newspaper picture?

Lesson 2 Review

Part A Write these Pattern 6 sentences on your paper. For each sentence, write *S* above the subject, *L.V.* above the linking verb, and *P.N.* above the predicate nominative.

<pre>
          S   L.V.   P.N.
</pre>
Example Sudan is a country in Africa.

1) Two popular Mexican foods are tacos and burritos.

2) Jupiter is the largest planet in the solar system.

3) Is Dan a friend of yours?

4) Who was that?

5) Lima is the capital of Peru.

Part B Write on your paper whether the word or words in bold in each of these sentences is a *predicate adjective* or *predicate nominative*.

1) *Romeo and Juliet* is a **play** by William Shakespeare.

2) The ending of the play is very **sad**.

3) Edgar Allan Poe was a **poet** and a story **writer**.

4) Warsaw is the **capital** of Poland.

5) Uncle David has always been **artistic**.

Part C Diagram these Pattern 6 sentences on your paper.

1) Janell is a good artist.

2) Be a responsible student and worker.

3) I will play the part of the unemployed singer, and Sal will be the owner of a small theater.

4) Are they the champions?

Part A   Write on your paper whether the verb in bold in these sentences is an *action verb* or a *linking verb*. Remember, a linking verb does not take a direct object.

1) Please **taste** the stew.

2) Does it **taste** too spicy?

3) This stew **smells** wonderful.

4) **Be** my pal, and help me clean up.

5) You **seem** upset about something.

Part B   Write these sentences on your paper. Write *S* above each subject, *L.V.* above each linking verb, and *Pred. Adj.* above each predicate adjective. Sentences may have compound parts or may be compound.

1) I am sorry.

2) My side of the room is rather messy, but my sister's side is extremely neat.

3) The day was cool and windy.

4) Aunt Pat is always happy.

5) Was she very angry?

Part C   Write these sentences on your paper. Write *S* above each subject, *L.V.* above each linking verb, and *P.N.* above each predicate nominative. Sentences may have compound parts or may be compound.

1) Are you the store manager?

2) He is my boss and my uncle.

3) Is she the one in the play?

4) Pablo and his family are our new neighbors, but Pablo and I have been friends for many years.

5) The last person in line was Jonas.

Part D   Write on your paper whether the word or words in bold in each of these sentences is a *predicate adjective* or *predicate nominative.*

1) Mariana seems **friendly**.
2) Sometimes she is **shy** around strangers.
3) Are you a good **cook**?
4) Leon will be a **senior** next year.
5) Last night, Dena was very **unhappy** about something.
6) She looks awfully **tired** lately.
7) Mr. Franklin is a creative **teacher**.
8) Rebecca and I will be **partners** for the project.
9) The weather has been **warm** and **sunny**.
10) For three months, the top salespeople have been **Santos** and **Ellie**.

Part E   Diagram each of the sentences. Beside the diagram, write whether the sentence is Pattern 5 (predicate adjective) or Pattern 6 (predicate noun or pronoun).

1) Her mother is a well-known lawyer.
2) That book will always be one of my favorites.
3) Spring is a nice time of year, but autumn is the best season of all.
4) The message was quite interesting and extremely important.
5) Will they remain friends after graduation?

Chapter

13

Complex Sentences

W hen you talk, you use all kinds of sentence structures. You do not even think about them. When you write, you need to be more aware of how you express your thoughts. You need to write sentences that make your meaning clear. This is because your reader cannot ask you to explain your ideas.

You know that a simple sentence is an independent clause. An independent clause expresses one complete thought. You have learned that a compound sentence has two independent clauses joined by a conjunction. You also know that a dependent clause is a group of words with a subject and a verb. A dependent clause does not express a complete idea. A dependent clause cannot stand alone as a sentence.

In this chapter, you will learn more about dependent clauses and sentence structure. This chapter focuses on different kinds of dependent clauses. You will learn how they are used to form complex and compound-complex sentences.

Goals for Learning

▶ To distinguish among a word, a phrase, and a clause

▶ To distinguish among simple, compound, complex, and compound-complex sentences

▶ To distinguish among adverb, noun, and adjective clauses

▶ To distinguish between a complex and a compound-complex sentence

Phrase

A group of words without a subject and a verb. A phrase relates to another part of the sentence.

Before you learn about complex sentences, it is important to recall the meanings of three important terms: *word, phrase,* and *clause.*

A word is a set of letters that has meaning.

A **phrase** is a group of words that work together. A phrase does not have a subject and a verb.

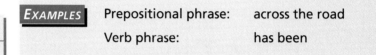

EXAMPLES	Prepositional phrase:	across the road
	Verb phrase:	has been

Clause

A group of words that has a subject and a predicate. A clause may be independent or dependent.

A **clause** is a group of words with a subject and a verb.

EXAMPLE	Clause:	**Unless there is a problem**

Activity A   Write on your paper whether each group of words is a *phrase* or a *clause.*

1) Over the river.

2) If he leaves.

3) Will have been late.

4) The youngest girl in school.

5) Whoever wants an apple.

There are two kinds of clauses: independent clauses (complete ideas) and dependent clauses (incomplete ideas).

An independent clause is a sentence. It expresses a complete thought.

Dependent clause

A dependent clause does not express a complete idea and cannot stand alone as a sentence.

A **dependent clause** has a subject and a verb, but it is not a sentence. A dependent clause is introduced by either a subordinating conjunction or a relative pronoun.

Remember that subordinating conjunctions are words like *because, if, when,* and *since.* Relative pronouns are words like *that, which, who, whoever,* and *what.*

 EXAMPLE   Independent clause: Marco walked home.

Dependent clause: Because he missed the bus

Activity B   Write on your paper whether each group of words is a *dependent clause* or an *independent clause.*

1) Whom you asked.

2) That girl is in my class.

3) Until he knows all the answers.

4) The team exercised before practice.

5) Whoever finishes first.

Activity C   Write on your paper the word that introduces the dependent clause in each of these sentences.

1) Because Shelly left school late, she missed the bus.

2) I will fix dinner if you are hungry.

3) Joey hoped that the band would win first place.

4) Rick admires the man who coaches his team.

5) What Angela said was not clear to everyone.

6) Since he didn't try out for a part, he won't be in the play.

7) We will start the movie when Tony and Maria arrive.

8) The witness told the police what she had seen.

9) Hank's Restaurant is closed while the owner looks for a new cook.

10) If that coat goes on sale, I will buy it.

Part A Write on your paper whether the word in bold in each of these sentences introduces a *phrase* or a *clause*.

1) We huddled in the cabin **as** the snow fell.

2) She won't be back **until** tomorrow.

3) Everyone has arrived **except** Jody and Bill.

4) I can't leave **until** I finish my report.

5) **When** you know the answer, raise your hand.

Part B Write on your paper whether the clause in bold is an *independent clause* or a *dependent clause*. Remember, an independent clause can stand alone as a sentence.

1) **After the party was over**, we cleaned up and went to bed.

2) Please take this to the woman **who lives next door**.

3) **I am so glad** that you made the team.

4) **This is the last time** that I give advice to anyone.

5) **Because the store went out of business**, many people in town lost their jobs.

6) Everyone stood up and clapped **when Stephanie finished her speech**.

7) Greg and the girl **who gives him a ride to school every day** live on the same street.

8) If you wait just a minute, **I'll walk with you to the bus**.

9) Peter took us for a ride in his new car, **which he bought himself**.

10) **Ask the girl** who is standing at the gate.

Adverb clause

A dependent clause that works exactly like an adverb in a sentence.

An **adverb clause** is a group of words with a subject and a verb. An adverb clause is a dependent clause that works exactly like an adverb in a sentence. It tells something about the verb.

EXAMPLES

Adverb:	Rick went home **early**.
Adverb phrase:	Rick went home **after practice**.
Adverb clause:	Rick went home **when practice was over**.

Activity A   Write on your paper whether the words in bold in each sentence are *adverbs, adverb phrases,* or *adverb clauses*.

1) Amy writes **well** and **often**.

2) Mom always knows exactly **where I put my things**.

3) **Except for you**, I haven't told anyone the news.

4) **Until you find your pen**, you can borrow mine.

5) I can hardly wait **until my birthday**.

Like adverbs, an adverb clause answers questions like *Where? When? Why? How much? How often?* and *How soon?*

EXAMPLES

Where?	Robin smiled **wherever she went**.
When?	**When practice is over**, Rick will go home.
Why?	Paula joined the band **because she likes music**.
How much?	Justin tried **as hard as he could**.
How often?	Mai practices the violin **whenever she has time**.

Activity B   Write the adverb clause in each of these sentences.

1) Enrique runs whenever he can.

2) If he gets up early, he runs in the morning.

3) He runs because he enjoys it.

4) Unless it is raining hard, Enrique runs every day.

5) Because I injured my knee, I walk for exercise.

An adverb clause may answer questions about another adverb. These clauses act like adverbs of degree. They answer questions such as *How much?* or *How far?*

EXAMPLE

S	V	D.O.	Adv.		S		V

Roberto hits the ball farther **than anyone else can hit it**.
(How much farther can Roberto hit the ball? farther *than anyone else can*)

An adverb clause may also answer questions about an adjective. These clauses are also adverbs of degree.

EXAMPLE

S	V	Adj.		S		V

Sam is taller **than the other boys in the class are**.
(How much taller is Sam? taller *than the other boys in the class are*)

Sometimes part of an adverb clause is missing. The missing part is understood.

EXAMPLES

Roberto hits the ball farther **than anyone else**.
(In the clause *than anyone else*, the words *can hit it* are understood.)

Sam is taller **than the other boys in the class**.
(In the clause *than the other boys*, the verb *are* is understood.)

Activity C Write the adverb clauses in each of these sentences. Add any words that are understood.

1) My dog can bark louder than any other dog on our street can.

2) Irene practices longer than anyone else.

3) Is Vicky taller than Beth?

4) Enrique ran farther than the others ran.

5) Charlotte is as happy as she can be!

Part A   Write on your paper whether the words in bold in the sentences are *adverb phrases* or *adverb clauses*.

1) Toni has been deaf **since birth**.

2) **Because she and Lisa became friends**, Lisa learned sign language.

3) **If you wish to learn**, Toni will help you.

4) Lisa had never signed to anyone **but Toni**.

5) **After she has been signing for a while**, Lisa will be good at it.

Part B   Write the adverb clause in each of these sentences on your paper. Add any words that are understood.

1) We will go to the beach when summer arrives.

2) Alexa bought a new bicycle because her old one fell apart.

3) You should get some rest if you are tired.

4) No one can run faster than Enrique.

5) That building is higher than any other city buildings.

Part C   Write these sentences on your paper. Add an adverb clause to each sentence.

1) Angie and her brother went to the baseball game.

2) Rain had been falling.

3) The field was wet.

4) The game began.

5) Angie cheered louder.

Noun clause

A dependent clause that works exactly like a noun in a sentence.

A **noun clause** is a group of words with a subject and a verb. A noun clause is a dependent clause that works exactly like a noun in a sentence. It may have a predicate nominative or a direct object.

EXAMPLES

Subject:	S L.V. P. Adj. **What you did** was wonderful.
Predicate nominative:	S L.V. P.N. That book is **what I need**.
Direct object:	S V D.O. I remember **what you said**.
Indirect object:	S V I.O. I gave **whoever wanted some** a piece of my pizza.
Object of preposition:	S V D.O. O.P. We made lunch for **whoever was hungry**.

A noun clause may follow any of the six sentence patterns that you learned about before.

EXAMPLE

      S   L.V. P. Adj.   V
Whoever is ready should begin.
(*Whoever* is the subject of the linking verb *is*. The whole noun clause is the subject of the verb phrase *should begin*.)

Activity A   Write on your paper whether the bold noun clause in each sentence is used as the *subject, predicate nominative, direct object, indirect object,* or *object of a preposition.*

1) The teacher said **that my answer was wrong**.
2) **Who will get the lead in the play** has not been decided.
3) They argued about **who should go first**.
4) This is **what I want**.
5) She offered **whoever was still around** a ride home.

A noun clause is introduced in a sentence by a relative pronoun.

Some Common Relative Pronouns	
that	who (subject)
what	whom (object)
whatever	whoever (subject)
whichever	whomever (object)
	whose (possessive)

The pronouns *that* and *what* have only one form. They do not change whether they are subjects or objects. The pronoun *who* does change, however.

- Use *who* when the relative pronoun is the subject of the noun clause.

- Use *whom* when the relative pronoun is the direct object or the object of a preposition in the noun clause.

- Use *who* when the relative pronoun is the predicate nominative in the noun clause.

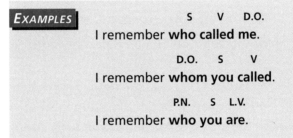

EXAMPLES

S V D.O.
I remember **who called me.**

D.O. S V
I remember **whom you called.**

P.N. S L.V.
I remember **who you are.**

Activity B   Write these sentences with the correct form of the relative pronoun.

1) I know (who, whom) called you.

2) I know (who, whom) you are.

3) I know (who, whom) you saw yesterday.

4) I know (who, whom) you invited to the dance.

5) I know for (who, whom) you bought that gift.

The relative pronoun *that* often introduces a noun clause. Sometimes it is left out of the sentence and is understood. Either way is correct.

> **EXAMPLES**   Correct: Do you think **that he is nice?**
>
>   Correct: Do you think **he is nice?**

The other relative pronouns cannot be left out.

> **EXAMPLES**   Correct: Did you hear **what I said?**
>
>   Incorrect: Did you hear **I said?**

Activity C   Write each of these sentences on your paper. Underline the noun clause. Circle the relative pronoun. If the relative pronoun *that* is understood, write it in and circle it.

1) Do you know who found my book?

2) Raina found the book you lost.

3) What I really need are my notes!

4) I am offering a reward to whoever finds them.

5) Do you think Raina found my notes, too?

Activity D   Write the noun clauses in each of these sentences on your paper. Beside each noun clause, write whether it is used as the *subject, predicate nominative, direct object, indirect object,* or *object of a preposition.*

Example   What I said was not important.
             What I said—Subject

1) I made supper for whoever wants some.

2) I knew that I would be late.

3) Some hot soup is what I need right now!

4) What you see is what you get!

5) The salesperson gave whoever was in the store a free CD.

Appositive

A word or group of words that renames or explains another noun in the same sentence.

An **appositive** renames or explains another noun in the same sentence. An appositive may be a noun, a noun phrase, or a noun clause. Look at each example below. The appositive is in italic. The noun that is renamed or explained by the appositive is in bold.

EXAMPLE   My **friend** *Anna* has a dog.

Meesh, *a toy poodle,* belongs to her.

Meesh's favorite **toy**, *a big rubber bone,* is under the chair.

I have a secret **wish**—*that I will someday be president.*

Activity E   Write the appositive in each of these sentences. Beside each appositive, write the noun or nouns the appositive renames or explains.

1) Do you know who wrote this line: "All the world's a stage"?

2) Carlo's big advantage, his powerful leg muscles, kept him going.

3) People laughed at Columbus's idea—the thought that the world was round.

4) The nineteenth constitutional amendment—the amendment that allowed women voting rights— changed history.

5) Herbert Hoover, the thirty-first president, was an engineer.

6) Galileo's invention, the telescope, changed scientific method.

7) The bibliography, a list of books used for reference, appeared at the end of the report.

8) The price was more than I—a student with no regular income—could afford.

9) Kareem, the editor of the school newspaper, is also class president.

10) Friends since kindergarten, Rita and Marianne still enjoy each other's company.

Lesson Review   Write these sentences on your paper. Underline the noun clause. Beside each sentence, write whether the noun clause is used as the *subject, predicate nominative, direct object, indirect object, object of a preposition,* or *appositive.*

Examples   Did you hear **what she said**?—Direct Object

Sue told **whoever was around** her news.
—Indirect Object

1) We went shopping for whatever we needed.
2) I think that you can guess the answer.
3) That love conquers all is a lofty idea.
4) A glass of lemonade is what I need.
5) Mrs. Garret gave whoever asked for it more time for the test.
6) She said she's tired.
7) When the paper is due is not clear.
8) Where he was going was not known.
9) I know where he was going.
10) A good map is what he needs.
11) He will go on an errand for whoever asks him.
12) Adam offered whoever was struggling in math class some help with math.
13) People laughed at Tom's belief—that he could win the contest.
14) Pay for what you want.
15) Is this what the dog brought home?
16) Seth forgot where he put his book.
17) Tell me who is coming.
18) How Sue did the job was important.
19) What she will do next no one knows.
20) She showed whoever wanted a peek her latest painting.

Adjective clause

A dependent clause that acts like an adjective in a sentence.

An adjective is a word that describes a noun or pronoun. An **adjective clause** is used in a sentence exactly like an adjective.

EXAMPLES

Adjective:	The **middle** girl is my sister.
Adjective phrase:	The girl **in the middle** is my sister.
Adjective clause:	The girl **who is in the middle** is my sister.

Activity A   Write on your paper whether the bold words in each sentence are *adjectives*, *adjective phrases*, or *adjective clauses*.

1) Terry is the player **who scores the most**.

2) The **best** and **most popular** player on our team is Terry.

3) The player **with the most points** on our team is Terry.

4) Ms. Nichols, **who has played soccer all her life**, is the coach.

Like an adjective phrase, an adjective clause follows the noun or pronoun it describes.

EXAMPLES

The book **that I gave him** was expensive.
(What book? the book *that I gave him*)

Are you the one **whom I met at the party**?
(Which one? the one *whom I met at the party*)

Jim invited Sandy, **who was his partner on the science project**. (Which one is Sandy? the one *who was his partner*)

Activity B   Write the adjective clause in each of these sentences. Beside each clause, write the noun it describes.

1) A girl whom I know won first prize in a contest.

2) The present that Gayle gave Susan was for Susan's birthday.

3) The answer that she gave was wrong.

4) The boy who sits in the first seat has been absent all week.

5) We bought a new refrigerator that has its own ice maker.

An adjective clause may be introduced by a relative pronoun. Some common relative pronouns are *who, whom, whose, which, what,* and *that.*

An adjective clause may also be introduced by the words *where* and *when.*

EXAMPLE The small town **where my dad grew up** is now a large city.

Activity C Write the adjective clause in each of these sentences. Underline the relative pronoun.

1) The band went to Florida, where a contest was held.

2) The contest that someone organized for high school bands is an annual event.

3) The director of the band, whose name is Mr. Smith, was very pleased.

4) The band, which had never been in a contest before, performed well.

5) We all hoped that the band would win first place.

Activity D Write these sentences on your paper. Add an adjective clause that describes the noun or pronoun in bold.

1) The bus took the band to **Florida**.

2) **Pedro** and Chris had a wonderful trip.

3) They stayed in a **hotel**.

4) **Everyone** enjoyed the warm weather.

5) The **contest** was exciting.

Lesson Review   Write these sentences on your paper. Underline the adjective clauses. Beside each clause, write the noun or pronoun it describes.

Example   Spring is the season <u>that I like best.</u>—season

1) Please get the bread that is baked at the grocery store.

2) Did you know the people who gave the party?

3) Mike is the one who plays right field.

4) The man whose brother drives our bus is very nice.

5) The outfit that Jenna wore to the party was new.

6) The girl who was in line behind me bought the last tickets.

7) The man who lived next door moved to Florida.

8) Sue's favorite actor is the one whom you liked in that movie.

9) Dwayne read the book, which Joanie suggested, in one night.

10) We rented a new apartment that had three bedrooms.

11) Nori showed me the notes that she had taken for the test.

12) Eduardo's uncle who is an airline pilot arrived in time for the party.

13) She was well prepared for the test, which she passed with a high grade.

14) The time when you should be thinking about your future is now.

15) I am the person whose book you found.

Sentences may be grouped according to purpose (statement, question, command, or expression of surprise). They may also be grouped according to one of many patterns.

Sentences may also be grouped according to structure. A sentence may be either *simple, compound, complex,* or *compound-complex.*

A simple sentence has one independent clause.

> **EXAMPLE**
> S   V   Prep. Phrase
> I will drive to school.

Complex sentence

A sentence that has one main, or independent, clause and at least one dependent clause.

A **complex sentence** has one independent clause and one or more dependent clauses.

> **EXAMPLE**
> S   V   S   V Pred. Adj.
> I will drive if you are tired.

Activity A   Write these sentences on your paper. Label the subject and the verb of each clause as shown. Then write whether the sentence is *simple* or *complex.*

>   S   V   S   V
> *Example*   The team was behind until José hit a home run—
>   **complex**

1) Every afternoon the baseball team practices.

2) When practice is over, the players are tired.

3) The team begins with warm-up exercises.

4) If they don't warm up well, injuries are likely.

5) Baseball is not usually played in the rain.

A complex sentence may have more than one dependent clause.

Adjective Clause

Richard Wright, **who was born on a plantation**, worked as a

Adverb Clause

dishwasher **before he became the author of *Native Son*.**

To find an independent clause in a complex sentence:

1. Identify the dependent clause or clauses in the sentence.

2. Read all the words that are not in the dependent clause or clauses. These words make up the independent, or main, clause of the sentence.

Activity B   Answer these questions about the sentence shown in the box. Write the answers on your paper.

> Richard Wright, who was born on a plantation, worked as a dishwasher before he became the author of *Native Son*.

1) What is the independent clause in the sentence?

2) What is the subject of the independent clause?

3) What is the verb of the independent clause?

4) Is the verb transitive or intransitive?

5) What are the parts of speech of the words in the phrase *as a dishwasher?*

6) What noun does the adjective clause describe?

7) What question does the adverb clause answer?

8) What are the subject and the verb of the adjective clause?

9) What are the subject and the verb of the adverb clause?

10) There are three verbs (or verb phrases) in the sentence. Which one is a linking verb? What word completes the idea in that clause?

A compound sentence has two independent clauses.

> **EXAMPLE**
>
> S   V   S V   P. Adj.
> I would drive, but I am too tired.

Compound-complex sentence

A sentence that has two or more independent clauses and one or more dependent clauses.

A **compound-complex** sentence has at least two independent clauses and one or more dependent clauses.

> **EXAMPLE**
>
> S   V   S V   P. Adj.   S V   P.N.
> I will drive if you are too tired, but it is your decision.

When you want to know how a sentence is constructed, analyze it. To analyze means to break something down into its parts. You can analyze a sentence to find out whether it is compound, complex, or compound-complex.

Here are the steps to analyze sentences.

Nick knows that a college education is important, but if he doesn't get a scholarship, he must wait until he saves some money.

Step 1 The independent clauses are *Nick knows* and *he must wait.* They are joined by the conjunction *but.*

Step 2 The noun clause *that a college education is important* is the direct object of the first independent clause.

Step 3 *If he doesn't get a scholarship* and *until he saves some money* are adverb clauses that tell about the verb *must wait.*

Step 4 This sentence has three independent clauses and two dependent clauses. This is a compound-complex sentence.

Step 5 These are the sentence patterns of each clause:

S   V   D.O.   Conj. S
Nick knows (that a college education is important), but if he
      V   D.O.   S   V   S V
doesn't get a scholarship, he must wait until he saves some
  D.O.
money.

Activity C Write each of these sentences on your paper. Find the independent clauses and the dependent clauses. Beside each sentence, write whether it is *complex* or *compound-complex*.

1) Mr. and Mrs. Johnson play golf when the weather is warm.

2) What I would like is a vacation.

3) Alicia works at the daycare center that is located next to the high school, and her sister works there, too.

4) Because of bad weather, the game was canceled, but it will be played tomorrow.

5) Both of us know that we must study hard, or we will not get into good colleges.

Direct and indirect quotations within sentences are noun clauses.

> **EXAMPLES**
>
>   S   V   **Direct Object**
> Mrs. King said, **"I enjoyed our golf game."**
>
>   S   V   **Direct Object**
> Mrs. King said **that she enjoyed the golf game.**

Activity D Change each of these indirect quotations to direct quotations. Punctuate your quotation properly.

1) Mrs. King said that she wants a new putter.

2) I told my boss that I could not come to work today.

3) Anita said that her mother was going back to college.

4) My brother Elvin whispered that he had a surprise for me.

5) Tina told me that she had found my book in her desk.

6) Matthew thought that we should go to a movie.

7) He said his favorite actor was Clint Eastwood.

8) He told his friend Jeffrey that he would stop by and pick him up.

9) Jeffrey said he would be waiting on the front porch.

10) Matthew told him he would be there in fifteen minutes.

The same idea may be expressed in different kinds of sentences.

EXAMPLES

Simple:	Ralph is a student and a part-time cashier.
Compound:	Ralph is a student, but he also has a part-time job.
Complex:	Ralph, who is a student, also has a part-time job.
Compound-Complex:	Ralph is a student, but he also has a part-time job that he has had since July.

Activity E Answer the following questions about the examples above. Write the answers on your paper.

1) Which sentence provides the most information?

2) What is the independent clause in the third example?

3) What kind of dependent clause is *who is a student* in the third example? Is it a noun, adjective, or adverb clause?

Activity F Write these sentences on your paper. Underline the independent clauses once and the dependent clauses twice. Then write whether the sentence is *simple, compound, complex,* or *compound-complex.*

1) After school gets out, Tanya hopes that she can find a summer job.

2) She asked Vic's uncle about a job, but he was not hiring.

3) She became discouraged about her job search.

4) Tanya kept on looking because she needed money for college, and she knew there was a job for her somewhere!

5) A person like Tanya who doesn't give up easily will look until she finds a job.

Part A Write on your paper whether each of these sentences is *simple, compound,* or *complex.*

1) I'd like to help you; however, I am very busy today.

2) Do you know what Willie said?

3) I think that I've seen that movie before.

4) The person in the middle of the line is my brother Willie.

5) Cliff said he was hungry.

Part B Analyze each of these sentences. Write on your paper whether a sentence is *simple, compound, complex,* or *compound-complex.*

1) Mrs. Huang planned a party for Kim because she was graduating from high school.

2) She invited Lisa, Elena, Cliff, and Enrique to the party.

3) Mr. Huang thought that Kim's friends should come to the party as their favorite person in history.

4) "It could be fun," Elena told the others.

5) The day of the party arrived, and everyone showed up at the Huang's house in costume.

6) Kim wanted a new watch for a graduation gift.

7) Because she was a swimmer, she wanted one that was waterproof.

8) Almost all good watches are waterproof today.

9) Kim went to the store with her friend Angie, and together they shopped for a waterproof watch that was not too expensive.

10) She found the perfect watch in the first place they looked, and she bought it.

Part A   Write on your paper whether each of these groups of words is a phrase or a clause. Remember, a clause always has a subject and a verb.

1) who planned the party
2) to the party
3) for Kim and her friends
4) that everyone will enjoy
5) because Kim is graduating
6) during her senior year
7) when you leave good friends
8) after so many years
9) after all her friends have gone
10) except for a few

Part B   Write on your paper whether each clause in bold is an *adjective clause*, an *adverb clause*, or a *noun clause*.

1) The person **who is planning the party for Kim** is her mother, but we said that we would help.
2) Alex, **who has already graduated**, has gotten Kim a present **that he purchased in Bermuda**.
3) The party will be held **after the graduation exercises are over**.
4) Mrs. Huang has planned a surprise for **whichever guest arrives first**.
5) **Whoever it is** will be surprised.
6) **Because the party is for Kim**, the guests will not expect a gift.
7) Mrs. Huang will prepare plenty of food **for whoever is hungry**.
8) Mr. Huang, **who is a great cook**, is making vegetable egg rolls.
9) **After the party is over**, Kim invited some of her friends for the night.
10) Their house, **which is quite large**, once belonged to a rock star.

Part C Read the sentence below. Then follow the directions and answer the questions. Write your answers on your paper.

> The gift that Mrs. Huang bought for the first guest is a CD.

1) Find the independent clause in the sentence. Write it on your paper.
2) Label the parts of the independent clause.
3) Write the dependent clause on your paper.
4) What are the subject and the verb in the dependent clause?
5) Is the dependent clause an adjective, an adverb, or a noun?
6) Is the sentence simple, compound, complex, or compound-complex?
7) Is the purpose of the sentence a statement, a question, or a command?
8) Write the sentence on your paper. Add an adjective phrase or an adjective clause to describe *CD*.
9) Add an adverb clause.
10) Write a sentence that follows the same pattern as the sentence above.

Part D Write on your paper whether each of these sentences is *simple, compound, complex,* or *compound-complex.*

1) What a wonderful time we had at the party!
2) We all enjoyed the food that Mrs. Huang prepared, and the music was great, too.
3) Who won the CD that Mrs. Huang bought?
4) Carrie and Mark came together, and they arrived first.
5) Mark said that Carrie could have the CD, which was nice of him.

Test Taking Tip When studying for a test, review the topics in the chapter. Then make up a practice test for yourself.

Chapter 14

The Verbal and the Verbal Phrase

The following sentences include verbals. "Writing a letter is a way *to talk* to a friend. The friend *receiving* your message will be happy *to hear* from you."

A *verbal* is a verb form that is used as a noun or an adjective in a sentence. The three kinds of verbals are *infinitives, gerunds,* and *participles.*

An *infinitive* is a verb form made up of the word *to* plus a verb. It is usually used as a noun, but it may be used as an adjective or adverb. A *gerund* is a verb form that ends in *-ing* and is used as a noun. A *participle* is a verb form that is used as an adjective. It describes a noun or a pronoun. There are present and past participles.

In this chapter, you will learn about verbals and their purpose in sentences.

Goals for Learning

▶ To identify and use infinitives and infinitive phrases in sentences

▶ To identify and use gerunds and gerund phrases in sentences

▶ To identify and use participles and participial phrases in sentences

Infinitive

A verbal that begins with the word to. *An infinitive can act as a noun, an adjective, or an adverb in a sentence.*

An **infinitive** is a verb form made up of the word *to* plus a verb. It is usually used as a noun, but it may be used as an adjective or adverb.

EXAMPLES

Noun:	I like **to swim**.
Adverb:	He practices **to improve**.
Adjective:	There was plenty of food **to eat**.

An infinitive is usually in the present tense. It can also be in the present perfect tense (*to* + *have* + a verb).

EXAMPLES

| Present: | Ella and Julian decided **to go** to the lake. |
| Present perfect: | They hoped **to have caught** ten fish by noon. |

Activity A   Write the infinitives in these sentences on your paper.

1) Ella and Julian really like to fish.

2) They hoped to catch enough fish for dinner.

3) Ella agreed to clean the fish.

4) Julian said he would like to cook the fish over an open fire.

5) Ella and Julian were on the lake by seven o'clock, ready to make their first cast.

An infinitive is not a part of the main verb or verb phrase. It may, however, be part of the complete predicate. Remember that the complete predicate is the main verb and all the words that describe that verb.

EXAMPLE

Verb   Infinitive   Adverb

Claudia / decided to leave early.

Subject   Complete Predicate

Activity B Write the complete predicate in each of these sentences. Underline the verb or verb phrase. Circle the infinitive.

1) Donna appeared to be happy.

2) Where do you like to go on vacation?

3) Sam seems to be taller than Fred.

4) Connie hoped to get the lead in the play.

5) Do you want to use the computer?

Do not confuse infinitives with prepositional phrases. An infinitive is *to* + a verb. A prepositional phrase is *to* + a noun or pronoun.

> **EXAMPLE**
>
> Infinitive: They want **to leave**. (*Leave* is a verb.)
>
> Prepositional phrase: Let's go **to the lake**. (*Lake* is a noun and the object of the preposition *to*.)

Activity C Write the words in bold in these sentences. Beside each group of words, write whether they are an *infinitive* or a *prepositional phrase*.

Example They wanted **to leave** early.
          to leave—infinitive

1) When Ella and Julian got **to the lake**, they saw other people ready **to fish**.

2) They carried their equipment **to the boat**.

3) Soon they were ready **to begin**.

4) Julian always wanted **to be** the one **to catch** the first fish.

5) "Do you hope **to beat** the champion?" Ella said **to Julian**.

6) "I hope **to catch** at least one big one by ten o'clock," said Julian.

7) They said hello **to the other boaters**.

8) "Look!" Ella pointed **to another boat**.

9) "That man just started **to reel** in his line."

10) "He will need a big pan **to cook** that fish!"

Although an infinitive is a verb form, it can be used as a noun, an adverb, or an adjective in a sentence.

Study each sentence pattern to figure out how an infinitive is used in a sentence. Ask yourself the same kinds of questions you ask to identify parts of speech and sentence parts.

EXAMPLES

Noun:	Julian wants **to catch** a big fish. (What thing does Julian want?)	
Adverb:	He will need a big pan **to cook** his fish. (Why does he need a big pan?)	
Adjective:	Ella had plenty of bait **to use**. (What kind of bait does Ella have?)	

Activity D   Write the infinitives in bold in these sentences on your paper. Beside each infinitive, write whether it is used as a *noun*, an *adverb*, or an *adjective*. Remember that subjects, predicate nominatives, and direct objects are nouns.

1) **To catch** a big fish was Julian's ambition.

2) His greatest hope was **to reel** in a big one.

3) After an hour, they decided **to move** to another spot.

4) They hoped **to find** a place with some fish.

5) They tried **to stay** cheerful.

6) The fish were hard **to catch**.

7) "Even a little fish would be nice **to see** right now!"

8) "Hey! My time **to pull** in the big one has come!"

Infinitive phrase

A phrase that includes the infinitive plus all the words and phrases that go with the infinitive.

An **infinitive phrase** is an infinitive plus any adverb, adverb phrase, or complement it may have.

An infinitive may have an adverb or an adverb phrase to answer questions about its action.

EXAMPLE	

Inf.   Adv. Adv. Phrase
To leave early for the lake was the plan.
(The entire infinitive phrase is *to leave early for the lake. Early* is an adverb that answers the question *When? For the lake* is a prepositional phrase that tells about *early*. It answers the question *Where?*)

An infinitive may also have a complement. It may have a direct object, a predicate nominative, or a predicate adjective.

EXAMPLES	

               Inf.   D.O.
He wanted **to find a job**.
(*Job* is the direct object of the infinitive *to find*.)

            Inf.   P.N.
She wants **to be the president**.
(*President* is the predicate nominative. It follows the linking verb *to be*.)

                Inf.   Pred. Adj.
They wanted the dinner **to taste good**.
(*Good* is a predicate adjective that follows the linking verb *to taste*. The infinitive *to taste* also acts as an objective complement that tells about the direct object *dinner*.)

Activity E   Write the whole infinitive phrase in each of these sentences on your paper.

1) Julian began to reel the fish into the boat.

2) The fish started to fight hard.

3) Julian's fish struggled to win the battle.

4) Ella got a net to help Julian.

5) To land that fish was their goal.

Sometimes the preposition *to* is missing from the infinitive.

EXAMPLES	

"Don't make me (to) **laugh**," shouted Ella.

Help me (to) **reel** it in.

Activity F   Write the infinitive in each of these sentences on your paper.

1) Will you let me help you?

2) They heard the other boaters cheer for Julian.

3) "Let us see the size of that fish," they all said.

4) They watched Julian hold his fish high in the air.

5) Their attention made Julian feel proud.

Activity G   Write the infinitive phrase in each of these sentences on your paper. After each one, write how it is used in the sentence.

Example   Their wish was to catch some fish.
          to catch—predicate nominative

1) It was time to go home.

2) They began to pack up their gear.

3) The sun was beginning to set.

4) Soon, it would be too dark to see anything.

5) To be on the road before dark was their goal.

Activity H   Write a sentence for each of these infinitives on your paper. Underline the entire infinitive phrase in each sentence.

1) to laugh

2) to rain

3) to be

4) to watch

Part A   Write the infinitive phrase in each of these sentences on your paper.

Example   The hours seemed to fly by.
to fly by

1) Ella and Julian wanted to be home by dark.

2) They decided to stop at six o'clock.

3) Ella began to count the fish.

4) They had hoped to catch many fish.

5) To catch enough fish for dinner had been their goal.

6) "How many fish are big enough to eat?" asked Julian.

7) "We have enough to feed your family and mine," answered Ella.

8) "I'll need a big pan to cook this one," Julian said.

9) "Let's get ready to go home," Ella said.

10) Soon, they were both ready to leave.

Part B   Write a sentence for each of these infinitives on your paper. Underline the entire infinitive phrase in each sentence.

1) to be

2) to work

3) to go

4) to find

5) to see

Gerund
A verb form that has an -ing *ending. A gerund is always used as a noun.*

A **gerund** is a verb form that ends in *-ing*. A gerund is always used as a noun. In sentences, gerunds act like nouns.

EXAMPLES

Subject:	**Drinking** and **driving** do not mix.
Direct object:	The dog began **barking**.
Predicate noun:	My favorite sport is **swimming**.
Object of a preposition:	The student got in trouble for **coming** in late again.
Appositives:	Ella enjoys two things: **fishing** and in-line **skating**.
	You might try the following kinds of exercise: **biking**, **running**, or **rock hiking**.
	Her special talents—**singing** and **dancing**—helped her get the lead in the musical.

Activity A   Write the gerunds in each of these sentences on your paper.

1) Riding a bicycle on back roads is great exercise.

2) I like running better.

3) My favorite activity is playing my trumpet.

4) She has trouble getting to school on time.

5) Finding his way through the strange city was a challenge.

6) They were sent to the office for walking in the halls without a pass.

7) His greatest goal was catching a big fish.

8) Talking to my parents can be difficult sometimes.

9) Dolores thinks fishing is dull.

10) She enjoys reading and going to the movies.

A **gerund phrase** is a gerund plus any adjective, adverb, prepositional phrase, or complement it may have.

Because a gerund acts like a noun in a sentence, it may have an adjective that describes it.

> **EXAMPLE**
>
>   Adj.   Gerund
> I get in trouble for **loud talking**.
> (What kind of *talking? loud.* The gerund phrase is the object of the preposition *for.*)

A gerund may also have an adverb or adverb phrase.

> **EXAMPLE**
>
>   Gerund   Adv. Phrase
> Rob likes **running in the morning**.
> (When does Rob like *running? in the morning. In the morning* is a prepositional phrase used as an adverb. The entire gerund phrase is the direct object of the action verb *like.*)

Because a gerund is a verb form, it may have complements.

> **EXAMPLE**
>
>   Gerund   D.O.
> **Riding a bicycle** is fun.
> (*Bicycle* is the direct object of the gerund *riding.* The gerund phrase is the subject of the verb *is.*)

Activity B   Write the gerund phrase in each of these sentences on your paper. Beside it, write whether the gerund phrase acts as a *subject, direct object, predicate nominative, object of a preposition,* or an *appositive* in the sentence.

Example   Getting ready for school is the hardest part of my day.
                 Getting ready for school—subject

1) Yori watched the running of the Boston Marathon on television.
2) One of his dreams was winning that race.
3) When he was very young, he began thinking about entering a marathon some day.
4) Yori enjoys two things: running and winning!

Don't confuse progressive verb forms with gerunds.

> **EXAMPLES** Verb phrase: Yori **has been running** every day.
> Gerund: Yori likes **running** every day.

Activity C   Write sentences on your paper for each of these verb phrases and gerunds. Be sure to use each one correctly.

Verb Phrases	Gerunds
1) will be starting	**6)** being
2) is beginning	**7)** finding
3) were going	**8)** running
4) has been trying	**9)** wishing
5) are planning	**10)** singing

Lesson Review   Write the gerund phrases in each of these sentences on your paper. Underline the gerund or gerunds in each gerund phrase.

Example   My hobby is collecting stamps.
               collecting stamps

1) Flying an airplane must be a thrill.

2) Reading books is a way to relax.

3) We enjoyed swimming in the lake.

4) An architect earns a salary by designing buildings.

5) My dog always gets in trouble for chasing cats.

6) The singing and dancing were good in that play.

7) I like cooking, but not cleaning up.

8) Finding anything in that messy room must be hard.

9) Locating a needle in a haystack seems impossible.

10) A farmer earns money by growing and selling food.

11) Knowing you has been my pleasure.

12) Some people enjoy weeding their gardens.

13) Planning our vacation was fun.

14) His favorite sport is fishing for trout.

15) Dana's hobby is reading.

Participle
A verb form that is used like an adjective.

A **participle** is another verb form. Participles are used in sentences as adjectives. A participle may be in the present tense or in the past tense.

EXAMPLES

Present tense: The **running** deer was beautiful.

Past tense: The house looks larger **painted** white.

He picked up the pieces of **broken** glass.

Activity A   Write the participles in each of these sentences on your paper.

1) The setting sun turned the sky red and purple.

2) Those cooked carrots are mushy.

3) The girl reading that book is my sister.

4) Will you help that lost child find her mother?

5) My rumbling stomach told me I was hungry.

6) The cracked glass hid the details of the painting.

7) Steamed vegetables are good for you.

8) The hikers climbed over the fallen log.

9) What a frightening movie that was!

10) Fish jumped in the bubbling brook.

Do not confuse a participle used as an adjective with a participle that is part of a verb phrase.

EXAMPLES

Participle: The deer **running** through the woods was beautiful.

Verb phrase: The deer **was running** through the woods.

Activity B   Write on your paper whether the words in bold in these sentences are participles used as *adjectives* or are part of the *verb phrase.*

Example   The **barking** dog scared the child.   **adjective**

The dog was **barking** at the child.   **verb phrase**

1)   Your cold is probably **catching**.

2)   We will be **catching** the train.

3)   The newly **painted** room was bright and cheery.

4)   They have **painted** the room a bright yellow.

5)   The wind was **howling** all night.

6)   The **howling** wind kept us awake all night.

Participial phrase

A phrase that includes the participle and all the words and phrases related to it.

A **participial phrase** is a participle plus any words that complement or describe it. A participle comes right before or right after the noun or pronoun it describes.

EXAMPLE	**Running at full speed**, she caught the bus. (The participial phrase *Running at full speed* describes *she.*)

Activity C   Write these sentences on your paper. Underline each participial phrase. Draw a line to the noun or pronoun it describes.

1)   Howling wildly, the wind frightened the child.

2)   Dana lent her book to the girl sitting in the first row.

3)   Expecting the worst, Julian was pleasantly surprised with his grade.

4)   The keys locked inside the car were of little use.

5)   Concentrating on her notes, Mrs. Agnello did not hear Julian enter the room.

6)   Mr. Agnello has mailed the letter addressed to the bank.

7)   Recommended by his teachers, Chan was given the award.

8)   Dinner cooked by her sons was a special treat for Mrs. Agnello.

Activity D Write the participle used as an adjective or the participial phrase in each of these sentences on your paper. Underline the participle in each participial phrase. Then write the word that the participle or participial phrase describes.

Examples   Running at full speed, the girl caught the bus.
<u>Running</u> at full speed—girl

The growling dog frightened the man and his son.
growling—dog

1) Walking to school, we passed a new apartment building.

2) Speaking in front of the class, Bobby got nervous.

3) Snacks are the only missing items in our backpacks.

4) The sleeping kittens looked adorable.

5) Swimming at the beach, we saw a shark.

6) Carol enjoyed the thumping sound of the music.

7) The book told a story about a sunken treasure.

8) Each of the patches on the hand-sewn quilt came from a piece of old clothing.

9) With his freshly scrubbed face, the boy looked younger.

10) Elena swept up the pieces of broken glass from the floor.

11) Trapped in an elevator, the girl cried out for help.

12) An adoring fan asked the rock star for her autograph.

13) The team, hoping for a victory, ran onto the field.

14) The skaters glided across the frozen lake.

15) I heard her chuckling softly to herself.

Part A   Write the participle or the participial phrase in each of these sentences on your paper.

1) We could see the boy running around the track.

2) The man found his lost dog.

3) Rowing rapidly, we soon crossed the river.

4) The broken bike could not be fixed.

5) Standing on the corner, we watched the cars go by.

6) Arriving early, we were first in line for tickets.

7) We waved to the marching soldiers.

8) I wondered who the girl walking by the restaurant was.

9) Totally lost, Dad still would not stop to ask directions.

10) Waving its tail happily, the dog stood and waited for its dinner.

Part B   Copy each of these sentences on your paper. Fill in the blank with a participle that makes sense in the sentence.

1) Denise handed out the _____ watermelon.

2) _____ to the hospital, we were almost in an accident.

3) I could not understand what the _____ note meant.

4) The woman _____ on the bench is my mother's friend Lily.

5) We had to throw away the _____ steak.

Part A   Write the infinitive phrases in each of the sentences on your paper.

1) Julian went to the graduation to see Elena.

2) "I am a little bit sorry to leave good old Wilson High School," said Barbara before graduation.

3) "It's a good excuse to have a party," Ella laughed.

4) We should find a place to meet.

5) "Let's plan to do that after the ceremony," Julian said.

6) Did you know that Sam wants to travel cross country this summer?

7) "To see Italy is my dream," Val said.

8) My plan, after I finish college, is to work in Spain.

9) Let's get together in ten years to talk about our accomplishments.

10) That sounds like fun to me, but I think we need to graduate from high school first.

Part B   Write the gerund phrase in each of these sentences on your paper.

1) Planning a party is always fun for that group.

2) "I enjoy playing charades at a party," Ella said.

3) For Elena, graduating from high school was a wonderful event.

4) After congratulating each other, Al and Billy looked for their parents.

5) Their actions—laughing and crying at the same time—showed that they had mixed emotions about graduation.

Part C Write the participle or participial phrase in each of these sentences on your paper.

1) Smiling from the stage, Sue received her diploma.

2) Roberto, walking across the stage, almost tripped.

3) With trembling voices, the graduates said good-bye to each other.

4) Someone handed a folded piece of paper to Elena.

5) She read the printed note and smiled.

Part D Write the verbal phrases in these sentences on your paper. Beside each one, write whether it is an *infinitive phrase*, a *gerund phrase*, or a *participial phrase*.

1) Standing in front of the school for a last look, the girls had tears in their eyes.

2) "Graduating from high school is something that you will always remember," said Mrs. Castillo.

3) As they drove away, Sue turned to take one last look at her school.

4) Shutting her eyes, Sue knew that she would always remember the good friends that she had made.

5) They all met at Elena's house to celebrate the graduation.

6) Elena had decided to invite all her friends.

7) Opening the door, she welcomed them all inside.

8) Everyone came in carrying food or soft drinks.

9) Barbara wanted everyone to sign her yearbook.

10) Looking around the room, Elena felt happy to see all her friends together.

Test Taking Tip

When taking a matching test, match all the items that you know go together for sure. Cross these items out. Then try to match the items that are left.

Glossary

A

Abstract noun—(ab strakt´ noun) an idea that you cannot see or touch (p. 13)

Action verb—(ak´ shən vėrb) a word that expresses physical or mental action in the past, present, or future (p. 80)

Active verb—(ak´ tiv vėrb) a verb that is used if the subject does the action (p. 105)

Adjective—(aj´ ik tiv) a word that tells about a noun or pronoun; it tells *what kind, which one, how many,* or *how much* (p. 54)

Adjective clause—(aj´ ik tiv klöz) a dependent clause that acts like an adjective in a sentence (p. 287)

Adverb—(ad´ vėrb) a word that answers questions about a verb, an adjective, or another adverb; it tells *How? When? Where? How often? How long?* or *How many times?* (p. 130)

Adverb clause—(ad´ vėrb klöz) a dependent clause that works exactly like an adverb in a sentence (p. 279)

Antecedent—(an tə sēd´ nt) the noun that a pronoun replaces (p. 28)

Appositive—(ə poz´ ə tiv) a word or group of words that renames or explains another noun in the same sentence (p. 285)

C

Clause—(klöz) a group of words that has a subject and a predicate; a clause may be independent or dependent (p. 276)

Collective noun—(kə lek´ tiv noun) names a group of people or things (p. 12)

Common noun—(kom´ ən noun) names a general type of person, place, thing, or idea (p. 4)

Comparative adjective—(kəm par´ ə tiv aj´ ik tiv) an adjective that compares one noun with another (p. 72)

Complement—(kom´ plə mənt) the part of a sentence that completes an idea (p. 248)

Complete predicate—(kəm plēt´ pred´ ə kit) the part of a sentence that contains the main verb and all the words that describe the verb; the main word in the complete predicate is the verb or verb phrase (p. 208)

Complete subject—(kəm plēt´ sub´ jikt) all the words in the subject; it may be one word or many words (p. 203)

Complex sentence—(kom´ pleks sen´ təns) a sentence with one independent and at least one dependent clause (p. 290)

Compound-complex sentence—(kom´ pound kom´ pleks sen´ təns) a sentence that has two or more independent clauses and one or more dependent clauses (p. 292)

Compound noun—(kom´ pound noun) a noun that is more than one word (p. 12)

Compound sentence—(kom´ pound sen´ təns) a sentence made up of two or more independent clauses joined by a conjunction such as *and, but,* or *or* (p. 215)

Concrete noun—(kon´ krēt noun) something you can see or touch (p. 13)

Conditional form—(kən dish´ ə nəl fôrm) a helping verb that puts a condition, or a requirement, on an action (p. 102)

Conjunction—(kən jungk´ shən) a word that connects related words or groups of words (p. 174)

Coordinating conjunction—(kō ôrd´ n āt ing kən jungk´ shən) a conjunction that connects words or groups of words that do the same job in a sentence (p. 174)

Correlative conjunctions—(kə rel´ ə tiv kən jungk´ shənz) a pair of conjunctions that connects words or groups of words that are related (p. 185)

D

Demonstrative pronouns—(di mon´ strə tiv prō´ nounz) pronouns that point to nouns: *this, these, that,* and *those* (p. 43)

Dependent clause—(di pen´ dent klȯz) a group of words that does not express a complete idea and cannot stand alone as a sentence (p. 276)

Direct object—(də rekt´ ob´ jikt) a noun or pronoun that receives the action from a transitive verb (p. 231)

F

Future perfect—(fyü´ chər pėr´ fikt) the verb tense that shows an action that will be completed before a certain time in the future (p. 86)

G

Gerund—(jer´ ənd) a verb form that has an -ing ending; a gerund is always used as a noun (p. 306)

Gerund phrase—(jer´ ənd frāz) a phrase that includes the gerund and all the words and phrases that are related to the gerund (p. 307)

I

Indefinite pronoun—(in def´ ə nit prō´ noun) a pronoun that refers to a noun that is not named (p. 46)

Independent clause—(in di pen´ dənt klȯz) a group of words with a subject and a verb; an independent clause expresses a complete thought and can stand alone as a sentence (p. 215)

Indirect object—(in də rekt´ ob´ jikt) a noun or pronoun that comes after the verb and before the direct object and usually answers the question *to whom, to what, from whom,* or *for what* about the verb (p. 241)

Infinitive—(in fin´ ə tiv) a verb form made up of the word *to* plus a verb; an infinitive can act as a noun, an adjective, or an adverb in a sentence (p. 300)

Infinitive phrase—(in fin´ ə tiv frāz) a phrase that includes the infinitive plus all the words and phrases that go with the infinitive (p. 302)

Interjection—(in tər jek´ shən) a word or phrase that shows strong feeling (p. 192)

Interrogative pronouns—(in tə rog´ ə tiv prō´ nounz) pronouns that introduce questions; *who, whom, which, what,* and *whose* (p. 39)

Intransitive verb—(in tran´ sə tiv vėrb) a verb that does not transfer action from the subject to an object (p. 231)

L

Linking verb—(lingk´ ing vėrb) a verb that joins the subject to a noun, pronoun, or adjective in the predicate; it is also called a state-of-being verb (p. 256)

N

Nominative pronoun—(nom´ ə nə tiv prō´ noun) a pronoun used as the subject of a sentence (p. 29)

Noun—(noun) names a person, place, thing, or idea (p. 4)

Noun clause—(noun klȯz) a dependent clause that works exactly like a noun in a sentence (p. 282)

O

Objective complement—(əb jek´ tiv kom´ plə mənt) a noun or an adjective that follows a direct object and adds to its meaning (p. 248)

Objective pronoun—(əb jek´ tiv prō´ noun) a pronoun used as the object of a sentence (p. 29)

P

Participial phrase—(pär´ tə sip əl frāz) a phrase that includes the participle and all the words and phrases related to it (p. 311)

Participle—(pär´ tə sip əl) a verb form that is used like an adjective (p. 310)

Passive verb—(pas´ iv vėrb) a verb that is used when the action happens to the subject (p. 105)

Past perfect—(past pėr´ fikt) the verb tense that shows one action completed before another past action (p. 86)

a	hat	e	let	ī	ice	ȯ	order	u̇	put	sh	she	ə	a in about
ā	age	ē	equal	o	hot	oi	oil	ü	rule	th	thin		e in taken
ä	far	ėr	term	ō	open	ou	out	ch	child	ᵀH	then		i in pencil
â	care	i	it	ȯ	saw	u	cup	ng	long	zh	measure		o in lemon
													u in circus

Personal pronoun—(pėr´ sə nəl prō´ noun) a pronoun that takes the place of a noun and that refers to a person or object (p. 28)

Phrase—(frāz) a group of words without a subject and a verb; a phrase relates to another part of the sentence (p. 276)

Plural noun—(plür´ əl noun) names more than one person, place, thing, or idea (p. 15)

Positive adjective—(poz´ ə tiv aj´ ik tiv) an adjective that describes one noun (p. 72)

Possessive noun—(pə zes´ iv noun) shows ownership or relationship (p. 20)

Possessive pronoun—(pə zes´ iv prō´ noun) a pronoun that shows ownership or relationship (p. 29)

Predicate—(pred´ ə kit) the part of a sentence that tells something about the subject (p. 208)

Predicate adjective—(pred´ ə kit aj´ ik tiv) an adjective that follows a linking verb and tells about the subject; completes the predicate (pp. 55, 256)

Predicate nominative—(pred´ ə kit nom´ ə nə tiv) a noun or pronoun that follows a linking verb and renames the subject (p. 265)

Preposition—(prep ə zish´ ən) a word that shows how a noun or pronoun is related to another word in the sentence (p. 154)

Prepositional phrase—(prep ə zish´ ə nəl frāz) phrase that begins with a preposition and ends with a noun or a pronoun (p. 154)

Present perfect—(prez´ nt pėr´ fikt) the verb tense that shows an action started in the past and continuing up to the present (p. 86)

Progressive form—(prə gres´ iv fôrm) the form of a verb that ends in -*ing* and uses a form of the verb *be* as a helping verb to show continuing action (p. 93)

Pronoun—(prō´ noun) a part of speech that takes the place of a noun (p. 28)

Proper noun—(prop´ ər noun) names a particular person, place, thing, or idea (p. 4)

R

Relative pronouns—(rel´ ə tiv prō´ nounz) the pronouns *who, whom, whose, which, that, what, whoever, whomever, whichever,* and *whatever* (p. 35)

S

-Self pronoun—(self prō´ noun) a pronoun that ends with -*self* and indicates action done to or by another pronoun or a noun in the sentence; -*self* pronouns are also used to show emphasis (p. 32)

Sentence—(sen´ təns) a group of words that expresses a complete thought; a sentence always begins with a capital letter and ends with a period, question mark, or exclamation point (p. 200)

Simple sentence—(sim´ pəl sen´ təns) a sentence that has one subject and one predicate and expresses a complete idea (p. 215)

Simple subject—(sim´ pəl sub´ jikt) the main noun or pronoun in the subject (p. 203)

Singular noun—(sing´ gyə lər noun) names one person, place, thing, or idea (p. 15)

State-of-being verb—(stāt ov bē´ ing vėrb) a verb that explains or describes the subject of a sentence; a state-of-being verb is also called a *linking verb* (p. 112)

Subject—(sub´ jikt) who or what the sentence is about (p. 203)

Subordinating conjunction—(sə bôrd´ n āt ing kən jungk´ shən) a conjunction that connects a dependent clause with an independent clause in a sentence (p. 180)

Superlative adjective—(sə pėr´ lə tiv aj´ ik tiv) an adjective that compares one noun with two or more other nouns (p. 72)

T

Tense—(tens) the time that the verb expresses in a sentence (p. 84)

Transitive verb—(tran´ sə tiv vėrb) a verb that shows action passed from the subject of the sentence toward a person or thing (p. 231)

V

Verb—(vėrb) a word that expresses action or a state of being in a sentence (p. 1)

Verbal—(vėrb´ əl) a verb form that is used as a noun or an adjective in a sentence (p. 299)

Verb phrase—(vėrb frāz) a main verb and one or more helping verbs (p. 82)

Index

Present tense, 84, 86
  commands in, 260
  infinitive in, 300
Price, possessive expressions of, 22
Progressive forms, 93–97
Progressive verb forms, 308
Pronoun, 1, 27–51
  adjectives and, 54, 140, 256
  defined, 28
  demonstrative, 43–45
  as direct object, 231
  indefinite, 46–49, 85
  as indirect object, 241, 243
  interrogative, 39–42, 205
  as main word in subject, 203
  nominative, 29–30
  objective, 29–30
  as object of preposition, 154–55, 164–65
  personal, 28–34, 232
  possessive, 29–30
  in prepositional phrase, 154–55, 164, 301
  as question, 39–42
  relative, 35–38, 277, 288
  -self, 32–33
  as simple subject, 203
Proper adjective, 60–62
Proper noun
  abbreviation of, 8
  capitalization of, 4
  course name as, 10
  defined, 4
  language name as, 10
  parts of country as, 9
  titles as, 11
Punctuation skills
  capitalization, 4, 8, 11, 60–62, 192–93, 200
  comma, 176–77, 192, 215
  with conjunctions, 177
  exclamation mark, 212–13
  hyphen, 12
  period, 212
  question mark, 192, 212
  quotation mark, 293
  semicolon, 177
  of sentences, 200

Q

Question
  pronoun asking, 39–42
  sentence as, 197, 212
    Pattern 1, 225
    Pattern 2, 235
    Pattern 3, 244
    Pattern 5, 261
  subject in, 205
Question mark, 192, 212
Quotation mark, 293

R

Regular verb, 86
Relative pronoun, 35–38, 277
  adjective clause introduced by, 288
  antecedents and, 35–36
  compound, 35
  interrogative pronouns vs., 39
  in noun clause, 283

S

Second person
  personal pronouns, 30
  plural, 232
  -self pronouns, 32–33
  singular, 232
-Self pronoun, 32–33
Semicolon, 177
Sentence construction, 196–315
Sentence diagram, 227. *See also* Diagramming
  sentences
Sentence patterns, 221–73
  with linking verb, 255–73
Sentences, 199–219
  analyzing, 292
  complete, 256
  complex, 197, 275–97
  compound, 197, 215–17, 225, 228–29, 236, 260, 268
  compound-complex, 197, 292
  coordinating conjunctions and, 174
  defined, 200
  incomplete, 256
  kinds of, 212–14
  with more than one verb, 80
  Pattern 1, 222–30
  Pattern 2, 231–40
  Pattern 3, 241–47
  Pattern 4, 248–51
  Pattern 5, 256–64
  Pattern 6, 265–71
  predicate of, 208–11, 234
  purposes of, 212, 290
  simple, 215–17
  structure of, 290
  subject of, 203–07, 222, 231, 241, 248, 256–57, 265
Sentence structures, 197
Series, commas in, 176